EDUCATORS FOR DIVERSE CLASSROOMS

A Case Study Approach to Equity and Inclusion in Education

Manu Sharma and Amanda Zbacnik

ROWMAN & LITTLEFIELD
Lanham • Boulder • New York • London

Published by Rowman & Littlefield
An imprint of The Rowman & Littlefield Publishing Group, Inc.
4501 Forbes Boulevard, Suite 200, Lanham, Maryland 20706
www.rowman.com

6 Tinworth Street, London SE11 5AL

British Library Cataloguing in Publication Information Available

Library of Congress Cataloging-in-Publication Data

Library of Congress Control Number: 2019950159

ISBN 978-1-4758-5110-6 (cloth)
ISBN 978-1-4758-5111-3 (paper)
ISBN 978-1-4758-5112-0 (electronic)

EDUCATORS FOR DIVERSE CLASSROOMS

I dedicate this book to my loving husband, Doron Yosef-Hassidim, and our beautiful twins, Keshet and Saagar Sharma-Hassidim.
I hope that this book inspires and ignites equity-based conversations in many teacher education programs, helping all educators become advocates for all students!

—*Manu Sharma*

CONTENTS

FOREWORD

Becoming a teacher is a complex process. At its best, teacher education connects educational theories and effective pedagogies to the experiences of aspiring teachers. By reflecting on these experiences, preservice teachers are better able to understand the learning process, the role of teachers in facilitating meaningful learning, and how to adapt pedagogy and curriculum to serve the needs of students within their schools and society. The personal experiences of aspiring teachers, however, tend to be somewhat limited.

Most teachers are white, middle class, and able, not to mention female, straight, and cis-gender. How then do they serve the needs of students who grow up with very different life experiences? How do they understand and, hopefully, come to embrace the diversity of their students, promote equity, and teach inclusively?

In my twenty years as a teacher educator, I have drawn on narratives and case studies as means to increase the breadth of experience of preservice teachers. Cases nested in the complexity of classrooms encourage them to exercise ethical and practical judgment.

In my professionalism and law classes, preservice teachers develop adaptive expertise as they apply pedagogical knowledge and critical-thinking skills to cases. In my social issues classes, case studies offer windows into the lived experiences of others while conveying the challenges of responding effectively in the moment. In practicum-related courses, cases help preservice teachers better read situations and adapt theory and pedagogy to address issues that arise within particular contexts. Such integration of theory, practice, and reflection is essential to the preparation of teachers able to adapt to a diverse and changing world.

Educators for Diverse Classrooms: A Case Study Approach to Equity and Inclusion in Education by Dr. Manu Sharma and Dr. Amanda Zbacnik is a very useful book for teacher education classes. The twenty-eight vignettes—brief narrative sketches of authentic experiences—cover a wide range of themes related to elementary and middle school education. These cases offer considerable food for thought regarding issues likely to come up in schools, such as dealing with exceptional learners, aggression, diversity, and bullying.

The cases developed by Sharma and Zbacnik offer rich descriptions of real-life situations along with a degree of ambiguity, as is generally the case for teachers in classrooms. The critical reflective questions guide one's reading of the cases while the academic literature connections readings offer opportunities to extend understanding.

More significantly, the vignettes serve as pedagogical tools for teacher educators seeking to encourage deep thinking about a range of equity issues and effective problem solving. These authentic stories invite preservice teachers to consider the opportunities and pitfalls of a range of approaches. Under the guidance of experienced teacher educators, preservice teachers have the opportunity to puzzle over ethical dilemmas and practical strategies relevant to cases and, by extension, similar situations they are likely to face during practice teaching or in their own classrooms.

The case study method encourages the integration of pedagogical knowledge across the teacher education program. Case studies such as these, by integrating theory, reflection, and practice, help beginning teachers develop inclusive teaching practices that address diversity and promote equity. Most helpful is the five-step analysis framework for analyzing the cases outlined in the introduction. These general questions will prove very helpful as guides to small-group and whole-class discussion.

These case studies are particularly valuable because they address dimensions of equity, diversity, and social justice. They open preservice teachers' eyes to different realities and generate empathy for diverse students. The vignettes raise social justice issues: What are the needs of the students involved? What are their rights and our expectations for them? They also prompt discussion of pedagogical issues: How does the teacher accommodate the student at the center of the story? How does she do this while ensuring learning and safety for all?

Through discussion of possible interventions, preservice teachers discover that there are several possible approaches. The choices they make will reflect their values. The process of working through the vignettes individually, in groups, and as a class will help them make more ethical decisions, as they increasingly factor professionalism and social justice principles into their deliberations and, later, their classroom practice.

I can imagine *Educators for Diverse Classrooms: A Case Study Approach to Equity and Inclusion in Education* being used in a range of teacher education contexts. The vignettes would be useful in units or courses focused on educational psychology, special education, classroom management, and social justice issues.

This collection would be particularly useful in a theory-practice course that connects theory and methods to the field-based practicum. This volume could also work well as a collection used across a teacher education program, with various cases picked up by different courses and others examined using more than one thematic lens. Beginning teachers able to respond to the situations sketched out in this book should be well prepared for the challenges they are likely to face in schools.

Julian Kitchen
Professor, Brock University
Ontario, Canada

PREFACE

In North America, K–12 public school educators are faced with ever-increasing diversity in their student populations. A majority of the time the identity of the public educator does not align with the rich vastness of diversity found in the student population they are teaching; as a result, there is often an unspoken discomfort about how to approach such diverse student populations.

The majority of our teachers are white, middle-class women, and the diverse population that they teach is composed of a variety of ethnic, racial, socioeconomic, linguistic, and ability identities. Sometimes, as a result of this discomfort and getting acclimatized to the teaching profession, educators are often faced with dilemmas related to colleague relationships, various levels of administrative support, challenges in establishing rapport with parents, considerations for physical classroom space, knowing when to submit a mandated report to social services, and how to best meet the needs of students requiring accommodations and/or modifications.

To address some of the above-mentioned circumstances, two assistant professors in the field of education, and with their personal experiences as educators, offer twenty-eight vignettes in this book to provide readers an opportunity to think through some of the challenges that educators may encounter throughout their early teaching careers.

To help analyze and facilitate the learning from each vignette, the authors provide a set of reflective and critical questions that highlight ethical dilemmas and topics for consideration, which are then followed by two to three academic literature connections that provide a theoretical underpinning to the topics discussed in the vignette. The hope of the set of critical questions and academic literature is to provide easier segues and multiple entryways into controversial discussions about each of these equity-focused vignettes.

In addition to drawing on the real-life case studies that present obstacles faced in the classroom, there is evidence that having students who are enrolled in teacher education programs reflect upon such case studies, prior to student teaching or establishing a classroom of their own, is beneficial. These case studies allow students an opportunity to gain the much-needed insight to feel confident in addressing issues that surface in their professional lives.

The students mentioned in these scenarios span the developmental age range of three to eighteen years, which lends itself to analysis of whether human development milestones are being met. The vignettes also highlight logistical complications that can occur in both urban and rural schools.

Given that the professional identity of a teacher is ever evolving and informed by practice and theory, teacher educators must guide students in teacher educator programs to reflect on controversial scenarios. By facilitating case study analysis, teacher educators can help their students to consider classroom management techniques that may need to be implemented to support all kinds of learners. Lastly, our society needs educators who are making decisions driven by ethical thinking, moral considerations, and legal responsibilities.

This textbook is written primarily for K–12 preservice educators, for all educators will be expected to embrace and learn together with diverse student populations with respect to their diversities rooted in but limited to their linguistic, ethnic, ability, racial, sexual, gender, and religious identities in their future classrooms.

The case studies, and prompted reflections, are also beneficial to all other professionals that work with individuals who have the honor to work with students in any capacity. This list includes, but is not limited to, social workers, school psychologists, mental health counselors, administrators, paraprofessionals, physical and occupational therapists, speech language pathologists, and parents.

Thus, the hope is that this book will help build future generations of critically aware and ethically minded professionals who will know how to support all our students, each other, and institutions through the myriad of complexities and challenges that are often posed in schools.

ACKNOWLEDGMENTS

I thank my friend and colleague, Amanda Zbacnik, for her amazing partnership in creating this useful and critical resource! I would also like to sincerely thank Julian Kitchen, Paul Gorski, and John Portelli, for their generous words about our book and their amazing mentorship. Finally, I would like to thank Joanne Bacon my editor whose patience and support has been invaluable.

—Manu Sharma

I would like to thank my co-author, Dr. Manu Sharma, for making this "pipe dream" a reality. I am so thankful to have met her at the University of Wisconsin's Faculty College, where we planned and put our goal of creating a case study book for preservice educators into action!

—Amanda Zbacnik

INTRODUCTION

Given the constantly changing student demographics in our public schools, teacher educators are tasked with preparing teacher candidates with reflective and critical teaching insights for reaching the needs and identities of all of our students. We contend that teacher educators can use controversial case study narratives to help encourage reflective thought on the ethical decision-making teachers face when dealing with complicated and sensitive issues in the classroom. This reflection can also help with practical insights on classroom management techniques and the development of problem-solving steps that may need to be implemented.

Outside of the classroom environment, these case studies provide an opportunity to reflect on professionalism and the relational aspects of collaboration among colleagues. Thus, we offer this short collection of twenty-eight case studies for teacher educators. We have also included critical case study questions that follow the narrative along with the additional resources that offer two research-based articles that teacher educators can utilize to further support their teacher candidate students.

In agreement with several scholars, including, but not limited to, Floyd and Bodur (2006); Hourigan (2006); Gunn and Williams (2015); Gunn, Peterson, and Welsh (2015); Bonney (2015); Smith, Boyle, Arbaugh, Steele, and Stylianides (2014); Brown and Kraehe (2010); Gonzalez-DeHass and Willems (2015); and Darling-Hammond and Hammerness (2002), we contend that case studies are a valuable teaching methodology in teacher education. Floyd and Bodur (2006) state that "[c]ase study analysis is an excellent way to bring issues related to students, teachers, and schools into college classrooms. Preservice teachers had the opportunity to analyze these cases collaboratively with classmates who offered multiple perspectives" (p. 58).

Similarly, Smith et al. (2014) and Gonzalez-DeHass and Willems (2015) share that the complexity of case studies help preservice teachers to dive into authentic classroom scenarios before entering into different classroom realities during field experiences and apply theoretical concepts they learn in courses in an applied context. Learning to respect and understand different perspectives present inside and outside of the case encourages students to engage in collaborative discovery.

To build on the beneficial opportunities that case study analysis provides to preservice teachers, Hourigan (2006) shares that we must emphasize the important role case studies play in helping develop reflective thinking skills. Moreover, Gunn and Williams (2015) and Lee, Summers, and Garza (2009) present a social justice–based argument for why case study–based teaching and learning opportunities are critical when addressing implicit or explicit biases and topics of diversity that exist in the case or in the case analysis process.

In light of this social justice lens, Gunn and Williams (2015) stress the importance of how students are prepared to carefully facilitate and analyze case studies collaboratively, whether it is between students or students and faculty in teacher education programs.

Given the social justice lens used in our case studies, we believe the implementation of case studies is just as, if not more important than, the content of the case study itself. We believe that the socially constructed knowledge that arises out of well-facilitated and well-prepared case studies is more effective than case studies that are not facilitated by critical questions from a social justice perspective, which might be couched in connections across a course's academic content (which is why we provide references to two academic pieces at the end of every case study) and the learning will not be as deep.

Moreover, we share the view of Gunn, Peterson, and Welsh (2015), who state, "[c]ase-based instruction is one method teacher educators can use to incorporate social constructivist learning principles and promote culturally responsive dispositions throughout content area coursework" (p. 68). Brown and Kraehe (2010) also argue that case-based instruction helps "build sociocultural knowledge by actively reflecting on their own experiences, while building new knowledge connections as they collaboratively engaged with peers, the course instructor, familiar cultural tools (e.g., scholarly research, media, popular discourse) and visual materials" (p. 324).

Furthermore, Gonzalez-DeHass and Willems (2015) also assert that case-based learning is a constructivist approach to learning given the sociocultural perspective that accompanies the context embedded in each case. Thus, we recognize that it is through the guidance of facilitators in decoding, analyzing, prompting, and scaffolding that the constructivist learning occurs. In the words of Darling-Hammond and Hammerness (2002), "[a] key lesson from these analyses is that cases do not teach themselves. Pedagogy in support of case learning matters" (p. 132).

Given the collaborative co-constructing knowledge opportunities case-based learning offers and the collaborative nature of the teaching profession, it is clear why such a pedagogical tool is necessary to use in a teacher education program. Moreover, the "[b]enefits associated with this method of teaching include prospective teachers gaining an appreciation for the complexities involved in teaching, opportunities for scaffolding of critical thinking skills, students being involved in authentic learning experiences for teacher decision-making, and student motivation to learn academic content" (Gonzalez-DeHass & Willems, 2015, pp. 117–118).

While supporting the above-mentioned literature on the importance of case study–based learning in teacher education, our book takes the case study methodology one step further. We advocate for the usefulness of case studies in teacher education programs not just as a way to begin thinking critically about classroom issues but also in particular to start engaging in equity- and diversity-based dialogue informed by our students' lives and needs in today's political school climate.

Thus, this book contributes to an increased interest in the use of case studies in teacher education for creating awareness and addressing issues of social justice and diversity (Brown & Kraehe, 2010; Gunn & Williams, 2015; Lee et al., 2009).

With regard to addressing diversity in education, Gunn et al. (2015) argue that, first, "teaching cases appear to be a useful tool to guide the reader to identify and discuss multicultural issues"; second, "case-based instruction is a useful vehicle to discuss and challenge beliefs and biases preservice teachers hold towards multicultural issues"; and, third, "sociocultural theories can be used as a theoretical framework for scaffolding preservice and inservice teachers' multicultural dispositions and skills during case-based discussion" (p. 69).

This case study book is a unique collection of public school experiences from the United States and Canada. The two different geographic locations also provide opportunities for insight into how school policy and curriculum (partially) addresses or does not address equity issues in classroom settings. Given the changing political climate in the United States, case studies that raise the salient issues of race, ability, ethnicity, and first-generation students are helpful for teacher educators to address political tensions.

At the same time, the Canadian public school system is also struggling with issues of gender and sexuality with regard to proposed revisions to the health and physical education curriculum and addressing indigenous knowledge and identity in the public school spaces as a result of the Truth and Reconciliation Commission's 94 Calls to Action (Truth & Reconciliation Commission of Canada, 2015).

In addition, both US and Canadian schools are struggling with a rise in mental health issues among students. As a result, this unique collection strives to bring difficult but much-needed conversations about current equity issues in North America to the forefront through case studies, and we believe these will be helpful to the changing field of teacher education.

All the cases in this book were developed by the co-authors based on their professional K–12 teaching careers. Dr. Manu Sharma taught and worked as an elementary and middle school educator for the Greater Toronto Area for approximately nine years in a variety of teaching roles. The vignettes we wrote are based on teaching in Canadian and US public school environments, respectively.

Moreover, these vignettes present ethical dilemma moments and epiphany-based experiences in each of the case studies in this collection. We hope these case studies help to convey situations of uncertainty and complexity within different levels of schooling, which can then become a point of engagement for preservice teachers and an introduction into a world of teaching that mirrors the complexities of ethical and difficult decisions they must make as future teachers.

By presenting case studies from two countries, we hope to provide insights on how educational systems, in whatever context they appear, (un)consciously support, hinder, or create possibilities to support all students via curriculum and ethical decision-making in the classroom and engage with the power dynamics operating between different stakeholders in the education system.

Through the process of discussing and writing up these cases, we learned that both Ontario and Minnesota public schools struggle with addressing the needs of teachers to better serve (un)diagnosed students with special needs. Another interesting theme that arose in our discussions was that different equity issues presented themselves when comparing Minnesota and Ontario schools.

Most of the US-based vignettes were focused on diagnosed ability-based needs of students and subsequently on socioeconomic status and sometimes on racial identity, whereas most of the Canadian-based vignettes focused on undiagnosed students with special needs, religion, and social class. Additionally, the demographic makeup of students in the stories varied widely.

The Minnesota schools where Dr. Zbacnik worked contained largely homogeneous white student populations, which may be attributable to the high level of gentrification of neighborhoods and the complex tiered system of school choice in Minnesota (e.g., private, charter, public, and homeschooling). In the more ethnically, racially, and linguistically diverse Ontario schools where Dr. Sharma worked, equity and diversity conversations were at least acknowledged, greater action was required on addressing how to reduce inequities that marginalized students encounter in public schools.

To help readers of this collection, we have also categorized the case studies by level of schooling (i.e., elementary, middle, and high school) and then also recategorized by equity topics, including, but not limited to, class, special education status, ethnicity, and language. Finally, we offer readers five steps to get them started thinking through each case. We encourage readers to use these steps for each case study before answering the critical reflective questions because the steps will help the readers familiarize themselves with the contents of the case.

THE FIVE-STEP ANALYSIS FRAMEWORK

1. Identify the problems in the case. What kind of problem is it (ethical, professional, and/or legal)? Give an explanation to support your thinking.
2. Who are the characters in this story, and what are their perspectives based on what is shared in the vignette? Create a table identifying all the characters in the story and add two outside characters (e.g., parents and school counselor) that should be thought about as well with each inside/outside character's perspective stated.
3. What are the equity issues present in the vignette? Give an explanation to support your thinking.
4. How can the teacher and other professionals address the equity issues in ways that are considerate of the vulnerable person in the situation? Identify and briefly explain at least two or three practical ways to address the equity issue to support the vulnerable person.
5. Why is it important to address the larger issues (e.g., socioeconomic status disparities) and problems brought forth in this case? How do these issues affect our society, and how do they contribute to your understanding of being a professional who works with diverse students?

We hope that this collection of case studies based on real-life experiences can offer critical insight and deep reflective opportunities for teacher educators and their teacher candidate students. We contend that transformative learning spaces occur in teacher education and then ripple out into our public school system with our graduating teachers. We invite with excitement our fellow teacher educators, students, and researchers to engage with the case studies in this book in the hope of developing a fresh perspective toward understanding equity and diversity issues in public classroom spaces.

REFERENCES

Bonney, K. M. (2015). Case study teaching method improves student performance and perceptions of learning gains. *Journal of Microbiology & Biology Education, 16*(1), 21.

Brown, K. D., & Kraehe, A. (2010). When you've only got one class, one chance: Acquiring sociocultural knowledge using eclectic case pedagogy. *Teaching Education, 21*(3), 313–328.

Darling-Hammond, L., & Hammerness, K. (2002). Toward a pedagogy of cases in teacher education. *Teaching Education*, *13*(2), 125–135.

Floyd, D. M., & Bodur, Y. (2006). Using case study analysis and case writing to structure clinical experiences in a teacher education program. *The Educational Forum*, *70*(1), 48–60.

Gonzalez-DeHass, A. R., & Willems, P. P. (2015). Case-study instruction in educational psychology: Implications for teacher preparation. In M. Li & Y. Zhao (Eds.), *Exploring learning & teaching in higher education* (pp. 99–122). Berlin and Heidelberg, Germany: Springer.

Gunn, A. A., Peterson, B. J., & Welsh, J. L. (2015). Designing teaching cases that integrate course content and diversity issues. *Teacher Education Quarterly*, *42*(1), 67–81.

Gunn, A. A., & Williams, N. L. (2015). Using teaching cases to foster a culturally responsive literacy pedagogy. *Teacher Education and Practice*, *28*(1), 45–60.

Hourigan, R. (2006). The use of the case method to promote reflective thinking in music teacher education. *Update: Applications of Research in Music Education*, *24*(2), 33–44.

Lee, K., Summers, E., & Garza, R. (2009). Effects of case-based learning on preservice secondary teachers' multicultural attitudes: A mixed methods study. *Academic Leadership: The Online Journal*, *7*(1), 15.

Smith, M. S., Boyle, J., Arbaugh, F., Steele, M. D., & Stylianides, G. (2014). Cases as a vehicle for developing knowledge needed for teaching. In Y. Li, E. A. Silver, & S. Li (Eds.), *Transforming mathematics instruction: Multiple approaches and practices* (pp. 311–333). Switzerland: Springer International Publishing.

Truth & Reconciliation Commission of Canada. (2015). *Canada's residential schools: The final report of the Truth and Reconciliation Commission of Canada* (Vol. 1). Montreal: McGill-Queen's Press.

I

Equity Issue: Mental Health

I

THE MIDDLE SCHOOL GIRLS' BATHROOM

A Cry for Help?

Manu Sharma

This vignette draws attention to the mental health concerns that many middle school students may be encountering and have a difficult time expressing to their teachers. It is important for teachers to acknowledge the struggle many youth face and how it may emerge in unexpected ways that need to be ethically addressed by their teacher. The following is a case based on a grade seven student's experience and how her health and physical education teacher was made aware of the situation.

VIGNETTE #1: SHIRLEY

By the middle of the school year, Ms. Rinku had gotten to know my students much better. One of the students in grade seven had demonstrated disturbing behavior throughout the first half of the year. Her name is Shirley. The background of Shirley's story is a disheartening one. She came to the school with a thick student record file.

When Ms. Rinku had the opportunity to read her file, she learned of custody battles, violence in her household, and alcohol abuse. Shirley had transferred schools more than five times during her elementary school years. She had come to Rosa Parks Middle School after gaining a reputation for picking fights and bullying students who were both younger and older than she.

Now, Ms. Rinku had Shirley in her grade seven health and physical education class. She often participated in gym but rarely followed instructions and safety protocols. Ms. Rinku often gave her leadership opportunities so she could instruct others during mini-games of whatever sports we were playing. Unfortunately, these leadership role opportunities were not enough to help Shirley stay focused and engaged in gym class.

Ms. Rinku recalls a time when she pulled off the hijab of another female student during a mini-basketball three-on-three game. The girl with the hijab broke down in tears, and Shirley just laughed. Another incident occurred when she took all the equipment out of the equipment room to hit her peers who were sitting in their squads and were awaiting Ms. Rinku's instructions as to what they were going to do that day.

Both these incidences were reported and shared with the administrators in the school and with her homeroom teacher. Each of these incidents was followed up with phone calls home to Shirley's mother. The problem was that the phone number was disconnected and Shirley's mother was hard to locate.

The only glimpse of her mother was when she came to pick up Shirley early from school a couple of times throughout the first half of the year. Her mother would be wearing revealing clothing and would use foul language when communicating with school personnel and with Shirley's peers. Her hostile ways made it difficult to have a conversation with her about her daughter's misbehaviors.

The episode that really pushed the limits happened after the winter holiday break. Shirley had come back wearing hyper-sexualized clothing that drew a lot of attention from her peers. When Shirley was asked to wear the school's T-shirt and gym pants that were available to students at no cost, she refused. Shirley had become more confrontational than ever before.

None of Ms. Rinku's student–teacher rapport techniques were able to deescalate Shirley's confrontational manner. Ms. Rinku knew that the school's social worker had been working with her, but she also knew he was a male. Ms. Rinku was not sure how Shirley responded to him, as there were no further updates in her student record.

It was during the second week back from the winter break that Shirley displayed concerning behaviors that shouted for help. Before entering gym class, she had smeared her feces across the mirror in the girls' bathroom. Many students came back to the gym with faces of disbelief and disgust as they shared with me what they had witnessed in the girls' bathroom.

It is important to note that the girls' bathroom is physically separated from the gym. When Ms. Rinku asked the students how Shirley was behaving, they responded saying that she was naked and laughing hysterically. Ms. Rinku immediately contacted the administrators and made them aware of the situation, and she instructed the female students to no longer go into the girls' bathroom. Ms. Rinku was not sure how to further address this situation given Shirley's behaviors and the lack of support from the administrators in an underresourced inner-city school. This was an eye-opening experience in Ms. Rinku's first year of teaching.

CRITICAL REFLECTIVE QUESTIONS

1. What should Ms. Rinku do (if at all) to further support Shirley?
2. How can the administrators, with limited school resources and finance, respond to the first-year teacher's challenges?
3. What are some of the symptoms Shirley displayed that require an ethical response from Ms. Rinku?
4. What would you do differently in your role as the teacher, and why?
5. Do you think such a case is under the responsibility of the teacher?
6. When an incident happens outside of the direct classroom (gymnasium), such as in the school's bathroom, but it affects your student, how do you address it when you are in the gymnasium?

ACADEMIC LITERATURE CONNECTIONS

Poteat, V. P., Rivers, I., & Scheer, J. R. (2016a). Effects of childhood traumatic event experiences. In M. K. Holt & A. E. Grills (Eds.), *Critical issues in school-based mental health* (pp. 164–176). New York, NY: Routledge.

Poteat, V. P., Rivers, I., & Scheer, J. R. (2016b). Mental health concerns among LGBTQ youth in schools. In M. K. Holt & A. E. Grills (Eds.), *Critical issues in school-based mental health* (pp. 105–117). New York, NY: Routledge.

Reilly, N. (2015). *Anxiety and depression in the classroom: A teacher's guide to fostering self-regulation in young students* (pp. 133–155). New York, NY: W. W. Norton and Company.

2

PERSEVERANCE ASSOCIATED WITH AUTISM . . . OR INAPPROPRIATE OBSESSION?

Amanda Zbacnik

For many individuals with autism, struggling to understand the rules of social relationships is common. This vignette features an eleventh-grade student with autism in the unstructured areas of the school hallways, on the bus line, and trying to maintain an appropriate relationship with students of the opposite sex. The questions focus on helping students with autism realize and learn from situations where their social eccentricities went too far.

VIGNETTE #2: JOHN

For many school professionals working with John, there was a picture of an impulsive obsession for food and a deep desire to have a girlfriend. John was on the autism spectrum, was focused academically, and had to have limits placed on the amount of food that he could consume; otherwise, he would eat too many sweets that would make him sick. There were also times, in conversations, where he needed to be told to slow down, as he would get so excited about his topics. In addition, even when wanting to redirect a topic, the focus would come back to discussion of food.

His special educator, Ms. Brown, noticed a change in John's behavior between his tenth and eleventh grades. It should be noted that John was very close to his dad and his parents had just gone through a divorce. John's mother also had a new boyfriend. John, who was usually very pleasant, although overly talkative, was beginning to display instances of rage and anxiety. At one point, he got so angry that his mother mentioned his jumping out of a moving vehicle. It was after another incident, where John got inappropriately verbal and physically aggressive toward his younger sister, that his mother decided to take him to a mental health therapist.

In the school, John, all of a sudden, developed a fascination with a female student who was pregnant. He would follow her around and ask her if he could touch her baby. It was reported that John had a girl who was a friend who happened to ride his bus. One day, this female friend came to talk with me, stating that John had reached up her shirt and grabbed her breasts. The logic that he stated out loud was, "Well, you're a girl and you're my friend. So, I guess you won't mind if I touch these." This occurred while waiting in the bus lines after school. From these situations, the school team decided to really focus on conflict resolution and establishing healthy relationships, especially with those of the opposite sex.

More positively, John had the very important role of being involved as the school's varsity baseball team manager. He was also one of the school's biggest sports fans, and this was the perfect opportunity for him to release his need for excessive talk. During his senior year, John was crowned homecoming king, which marked a moment of acceptance by his peers. Lastly, it was Ms. Brown's hope that John would bring his energy to the workplace or whatever goals he chose to pursue.

CRITICAL REFLECTIVE QUESTIONS

1. Having an intense interest or obsession with certain topics or items is a common characteristic for individuals with autism. Share your opinion about how John's obsession could be worked into his educational curriculum. Or, in your opinion, should this topic be included in a minimal fashion?
2. High school, and even middle school, is a time where students are beginning to establish intimate relationships with the opposite or same sex. In response to the situations, displaying confusion about

how to establish healthy relationships, are there social stories or narratives that could be developed to help John understand the appropriate ways to interact with females?

3. How important is peer acceptance?

ACADEMIC LITERATURE CONNECTIONS

Lequia, J. (2011). Motivation, interest, and attention: Re-defining learning in the autism spectrum? *International Journal of Disability, Development and Education, 58*(4), 405–408.

Ranson, N., & Byrne, M. (2014). Promoting peer acceptance of females with higher-functioning autism in a mainstream education setting: A replication and extension of the effects of an autism anti-stigma program. *Journal of Autism and Developmental Disorders, 44*(11), 2278–2796.

II

Equity Issue: Special Education Concerns

3

A DOWNWARD SPIRAL

Frustration Takes over Parent, Teacher,
and Student Relationships

Manu Sharma

This vignette draws attention to how high-functioning students with autism spectrum disorder (ASD) in a middle school setting may experience depression. Moreover, this narrative shares the implications ASD has on parents of children who have ASD. It is essential for teachers to be mindful that parents sometimes need extra attention as they are still learning to cope and work with their child's ASD.

However, at the same time, it is important to draw some boundaries between how much the parent input or demands can influence a teacher's autonomy in teaching the students in his or her class. The following is a case based on a grade six student's experience and how his Home School Program teacher had to decide how to ethically address the parents' and student's needs.

VIGNETTE #3: PABLO

In Woodland, a midsized middle school, a small grade six Home School Program (HSP) ran to meet the needs of students who are two to three years behind their expected grade level. In this HSP classroom, there were eight students. Each of these students had a range of needs in addition to their academic performance needs. This HSP was partially integrated because its students participated in music, drama, and physical education classes with the mainstream classes.

One of the students, named Pablo, displayed many symptoms of what appeared to be depression. Pablo would often avoid social interaction, such as eye contact, and kept his head down throughout the class. The teacher of the HSP, Ms. Frost, felt the need to collaborate with Pablo's parents and the rotary art-based teachers. Ms. Frost set up a preliminary meeting with Pablo's parents. As a result, Pablo's mother, Karen, came in by herself and met Ms. Frost because Pablo's father was away for a business trip.

Karen was overly involved with Pablo's every need. This was apparent because, at the meeting, she began to talk about her challenges raising Pablo. She explained how Pablo would throw tantrums in kindergarten and refuse to go to school. Karen felt that something was different with Pablo, so she took him to several psychologists to have him assessed. However, the waitlist to see a psychologist was often too long, and she was unable to get her son assessed before grade five.

With excitement, she shared with Ms. Frost that Pablo was finally assessed the summer before he came to Woodland. The result of the assessment was that Pablo was further along the autism spectrum than previously thought. He was in the moderate level of ASD.

She went on to say that she felt relieved that Ms. Frost took the time to learn and hear about Pablo's assessment. Unfortunately, Karen did not address Ms. Frost's concerns about Pablo's depression-like symptoms. When the meeting came to a close, Ms. Frost thanked Karen and suggested that she should meet with and update the principal about Pablo's assessment.

After one month of reading up on how to work and engage with students who struggle with ASD, Ms. Frost was eager to implement these strategies for Pablo in class. Ms. Frost tried to scaffold tasks for Pablo in class and provide him with frequent breaks during which he could play school board–approved video games. Pablo was unable to complete the scaffolded tasks because he preferred to remain disengaged and removed from the class activities.

Ms. Frost then tried to provide a separate schedule for Pablo in which he could complete tasks based on his interests. As a result, he showed a little interest, but his depression-like symptoms were still evident. Pablo would put his head down on the table and refuse to engage with anyone.

Concerned about these behaviors, Ms. Frost set up a follow-up meeting with Karen.

Karen, who had learned from Pablo about Ms. Frost's new strategies, came in the next morning and handed Ms. Frost a thick book on ASD. As Karen handed the book to Ms. Frost, she yelled at her and said that "as a teacher she should get her act together before attempting to educate her son." Shocked, Ms. Frost gently explained that she had been researching and learning about ASD and, as a result, had implemented many strategies, such as noise-canceling headphones, a quiet setting, scaffolded tasks, a personalized schedule, and a reward system, but none of these accommodations seemed to be helping Pablo improve his academic performance.

As a result, Karen became defensive and said, "Maybe my son is depressed because you do not know how to teach him." Karen then headed toward the principal's office. Later in the morning, Ms. Frost was asked to meet with the principal. Ms. Frost became very nervous because this was only her second year being a special education teacher. She sat down across from the principal and listened to the principal explaining the importance of keeping parents happy. The principal told Ms. Frost that she was to follow and fulfill all of Karen's requests. Moreover, the principal did not want to hear about this situation again.

The next morning, Karen arrived with a long list of requests, which included her demand that all of Pablo's tasks be color coordinated, all his homework be written in the agenda, he have full access to an iPad throughout the class, and Ms. Frost should call Karen every day after school. During the phone call, Ms. Frost was to provide a detailed report on what Pablo accomplished, a daily reflection on his emotional behavior, and a list of students with which he interacted during HSP and integrated classes.

After reading loudly this long list of requests in front of students who were entering the class just as the bell rang, Karen said, "Now, that I have spelled out and said it out loud, do you think you can make your incompetent mind work and meet the needs of my child? I hope you can; otherwise, I will be back with the principal." Ms. Frost started to tear up, looked at her students, and wondered how this day would go. She stood silent in front of Karen, frozen, without knowing what to say.

CRITICAL REFLECTIVE QUESTIONS

1. What would you do if you were Ms. Frost at the end of the story, facing Karen?
2. Where could further support have been found for Pablo, Karen, Ms. Frost, and the principal?
3. Is there a boundary between how much individualized attention and focus can be given to one student in a high-needs special education class?
4. How was Ms. Frost's engagement with Pablo disruptive to the learning of other students in the class?
5. When should parents' and principals' needs and desires take priority over teachers' insights?

ACADEMIC LITERATURE CONNECTIONS

Gadow, K. D., Guttmann-Steinmetz, S., Rieffe, C., & DeVincent, C. J. (2012). Depression symptoms in boys with autism spectrum disorder and comparison samples. *Journal of Autism and Developmental Disorders, 42*(7), 1353–1363.

Greenlee, J. L., Mosley, A. S., Shui, A. M., Veenstra-VanderWeele, J., & Gotham, K. O. (2016). Medical and behavioral correlates of depression history in children and adolescents with autism spectrum disorder. *Pediatrics, 137*(Suppl. 2), S105–S114.

Weitlauf, A. S., Vehorn, A. C., Taylor, J. L., & Warren, Z. E. (2014). Relationship satisfaction, parenting stress, and depression in mothers of children with autism. *Autism, 18*(2), 194–198.

4

TEACHER AND STUDENT FRIENDSHIP FOR THE SAKE OF MAKING PROGRESS IN READING

Manu Sharma

This vignette showcases the vulnerability of a student with special learning needs whose academic learning goals are supported by a teacher who goes out of her way to help this easily distracted student. The teacher's actions ask the reader to contemplate the level of professionalism involved from an outsider's perspective. Another point of consideration this case makes is to consider when a principal, who chooses to focus on life skills instead, redirects academic goals. This narrative then exposes the reader to various perspectives on importance (or lack of importance) of academic goals for a grade six student with special needs.

VIGNETTE #4: TAMMY

It was the first day of school at Hayden Park Public Middle School. Ms. Trinity was busy preparing her special education classroom for students who were one to two years behind in their academic achievement. This special education program was called the Home School Program. Ms. Trinity had six students in this class. One of the new students was Tammy, a young African American who had a great deal of enthusiasm for life and passion for fashion!

Tammy enjoyed hands-on tasks and had not developed a love for reading because she had struggled with it for several years in elementary school. Ms. Trinity hoped that she could turn that struggle around and have Tammy fall in love with reading. She did a great deal of background research on Tammy's interests by speaking with Tammy and Tammy's mother.

Ms. Trinity had learned that Tammy enjoyed arts and crafts in addition to her flair for fashion. Therefore, Ms. Trinity ordered some books on these topics for Tammy from the local library to help her get reinterested in reading. Tammy had started to make progress, and she decided to take the books home to read and promised Ms. Trinity that she would read for five minutes a day.

By mid-September she had decided to start reading for fifteen minutes a day, and this was because she had an opportunity to speak with Ms. Trinity about her books every day in the Home School classroom. By October Tammy had started enjoying the routine of taking home a book, reading it, coming back the next day, and sharing what she had learned with Ms. Trinity. As a result of being very proud of Tammy, Ms. Trinity shared Tammy's progress in engaging with reading again with the school principal, Ms. Burns, and Tammy's mother.

As the first semester continued, Tammy showed a great deal of improvement not only in her reading but also in her reading comprehension. In order to develop deep thinking, Ms. Trinity gave Tammy scaffolded tasks about mysteries that involved fashion crimes. For example, a series of tasks would include a quick retelling of the mystery, an opportunity to respond to prediction questions, identifying elements of the story that may need to be further examined, and any further questions Tammy had about the story. As a new student, Tammy had quickly excelled in the Home School Program.

During the integrated component of the program, Tammy had an opportunity to interact and socialize with peers in grade six. Around November, Tammy had shared with Ms. Trinity that she had developed a crush on a boy named Blair who was in the integrated music class. She also shared that Blair was not interested in her because he was busy pursuing another girl named Samantha.

Samantha was in the same music class as Blair and Tammy. Samantha had developed a reputation in school for singing beautifully but also for not completing her work and not caring about her grades. As a result, Tammy felt she needed to become more like Samantha and started to let her reading progress slip.

Noticing the change in Tammy's attitude, Ms. Trinity shared with Tammy that it is important to keep up with her reading progress to not ruin her potential to succeed in school. Ms. Trinity spoke with Tammy's mother as well and learned that Tammy was giving her a hard time at home and even began demonstrating disrespect toward her mother. Evaluating the situation, Ms. Trinity offered friendship to Tammy in the hopes of guiding her back to keeping up with her reading while at the same time supporting her pursuit of Blair.

As the weeks progressed, Tammy started asking to spend time with Ms. Trinity outside of school. Tammy had asked Ms. Trinity to go shopping with her for sexy and stylish clothes, as her mother did not approve of her buying such clothes. Ms. Trinity felt uncomfortable but was torn, as she knew that, if she were to set a boundary on their friendship, Tammy would stop actively participating in her class. Ms. Trinity avoided answering Tammy's request for shopping for a week. After a long weekend of turmoil, Ms. Trinity decided to tell the principal, Ms. Burns, what was going on.

Consequently, the following morning Ms. Burns decided to pull Tammy out of Ms. Trinity's class and give her tasks to do in the administrative office. Ms. Burns has created a schedule to keep Tammy busy from the beginning to the end of the school day. Tammy was to do the morning and afterschool announcements, organize the principal's books and clean up the office, and help deliver school supplies to classrooms as needed.

Beyond the simple tasks, Tammy was asked to sit down and read by herself and no longer participate in the Home School Program or the integrated music class. When Ms. Trinity realized how little educational opportunities Tammy was given, she asked Ms. Burns whether pulling Tammy out of the Home School Program was beneficial to her academic progress.

Ms. Burns took a deep breath and said, "Education comes in many forms, and students like Tammy need to be kept busy before they get into trouble. Moreover, the organizational and vocal skills are Tammy's strong skills, and they provide the most hope for her future as a secretary." Ms. Trinity was appalled by these remarks made by the principal. She had no idea how to make this difficult situation better.

CRITICAL REFLECTIVE QUESTIONS

1. When is it okay (if at all) for a teacher to become a friend of a student who is not achieving academic success? Why?
2. Do you think it was acceptable for Ms. Burns to pull Tammy out of Ms. Trinity's class? Please explain why.
3. What do you think about Ms. Burns's schedule for Tammy? Do you think this schedule has any biases in it?
4. Why is Ms. Trinity unsure how to proceed in this situation at the end of the story? What would you do if you were Ms. Trinity?
5. How should this new schedule for Tammy be communicated with Tammy's mother? Whose duty is it to inform Tammy's mother?

ACADEMIC LITERATURE CONNECTIONS

Kauffman, J. M., Hallahan, D. P., Pullen, P. C., & Badar, J. (2018). *Special education: What it is and why we need it* (chapters 3 and 4). New York, NY: Routledge.
Professional development on trauma-sensitive schools: http://dpi.wi.gov/sspw/mental-health/trauma

5

UNDERSTANDING STUDENTS' PHYSICAL LIMITATIONS

When Should a Paraprofessional Assist with Mobility Safety Needs?

Amanda Zbacnik

This vignette examines the complexity of a particular type of muscular dystrophy and precautions that need to be taken for a second grade student with this orthopedic impairment at recess and in physical therapy. The decision to hire a paraprofessional may also be needed to assist with stretching and helping the individual understand his or her physical limits.

VIGNETTE #5: SHAWN

Shawn was a second-grade boy who had Duchene's muscular dystrophy, which made walking extremely challenging for him. Shawn's best buddy was Nicole, who was into being active. So, as you can imagine, this presented some challenges for Shawn in trying to physically keep up with her. Sometimes, students with muscular dystrophy do not have any intellectual disabilities, but Shawn was in the 80 percent who do have some cognitive limitations. In his mind, trying to keep up with Nicole was perfectly acceptable.

Little did he understand that he lacked the judgment to know when he was physically pushing himself too hard. Shawn was always willing to try

new things. He was a good friend to many of the students in the classroom. Underestimating his physical limitations was the biggest barrier for
Shawn. He would often go outside at recess and had struggles maneuver-
ing over the different surface areas that existed on the playground (grassy
hillsides, woodchips, securing himself on a swing, or transitioning from
woodchips to the sidewalk).

The IEP team decided it was best to hire a paraprofessional to help
Shawn with his mobility due to safety considerations and to assist in
completing his physical therapy stretches to strengthen his muscles. The
challenging aspect about muscular dystrophy is that it causes muscles to
deteriorate, so there was great need for a physical therapist (PT). The
school district was blessed with an amazing PT. He was able to match
Shawn up with some ankle guards and leg braces that would help his
walking.

For safety purposes, the PT also recommended that Shawn have a
harness around his midsection while walking or playing on the playground. The harness was something that the paraprofessional could
quickly hold onto should Shawn be on the edge of toppling over. The
ability to work his muscles, with limited fear of falling, helps slow down
the progressive disease. This provided an alternate to being in a walker
and then ending up in a wheelchair.

Shawn's mother had the carrier gene for muscular dystrophy and so
did her sister, so Shawn had an older cousin in the same school who also
had muscular dystrophy. Thinking about the occurrence of this disease,
Ms. Brown, Shawn's teacher, was able to picture Shawn in the earlier
stages of muscular dystrophy and his older cousin who had to be in a
wheelchair as signifying the progression of the disease.

Shawn and his older cousin had to go to multiple medical visits
throughout the year to have biopsies done of their muscles. At times, this
would include prednisone shots and, of course, the daily ritual of doing
the physical therapy stretches. These stretches were something that was a
bit uncomfortable to do every day but in the long run would improve the
longevity of his muscles and, ultimately, his life.

CRITICAL REFLECTIVE QUESTIONS

1. Think about your ideal classroom setup. What sort of considerations would need to be made to make all areas of the classroom accessible to a student like Shawn, with limited mobility?
2. Frequent visits to the hospital are part of the personal care process for individuals with muscular dystrophy. As a classroom teacher, what type of plan could be arranged to ensure that Shawn has access to the general education instruction being taught during his hospitalization?

ACADEMIC LITERATURE CONNECTIONS

Hopkins, L. (2016). Hospital-based education support for students with chronic health conditions. *Australian Health Review, 40*(2), 213–218.

Pivik, J., McComas, J., & Laflamme, M. (2002). Barriers and facilitators to inclusive education. *Exceptional Children, 69*(1), 97–107.

6

ROUTINES AND SELF-REGULATION

A Preference or a Necessity?

Amanda Zbacnik

This vignette highlights the challenge to understand the neurological need of a second-grade boy with autism in the special education classroom and cafeteria. For many individuals with autism, insistence on routine and sensitivity to sensory elements are very commonplace. However, this case also gets educators thinking about ways to identify whether resistance to new topics of learning is part of a child with autism's disability or strong-willed nature.

VIGNETTE #6: HERMAN

Herman was a second-grade boy with autism who would get quite angry due to having limited communication skills. He had fantastic intellectual capabilities and would quickly get through academic tasks. From there, he would engage in free choice activities as a reward. This "first/then" sequence was used quite a bit. However, occasionally there were tasks that Herman absolutely refused to complete.

When in the "refusal mode," Herman was the child that could make or break their entire environment and atmosphere in the special education room. His behaviors included high-pitched screaming; engaging in self-inflicted injuries, such as hitting his head against the wall; or seeking other students to push before dropping to the ground. Luckily for Herman, he had a very consistent yet firm paraprofessional that he worked with.

The underlying issue was that Herman could not effectively communicate his frustration, so the paraprofessional went to speech-language pathologist sessions with Herman and worked closely with me to develop a picture exchange communication system. This system began working excellently for helping Herman understand his routine for the day and in offering certain choices for work well done.

The experience with Herman helped Ms. Brown understand the importance of offering choice (as a motivator) and the importance of establishing routine (via pictures) for students with autism spectrum disorder (ASD). The next aspect that needed to be addressed was a way for Herman to regulate his behaviors. As for many students with ASD, Herman displayed the need for gross motor sensory integration.

Herman would spend twenty minutes of his day (ten minutes in the morning and ten minutes in the afternoon) in a large swing that we had bolstered to the ceiling of the classroom. This decision was critical for Herman to have a successful day at school. His IEP team members also needed to adjust his schedule to be more varied in terms of fine and gross motor activity.

The last glimpse into autism, learned from Herman, had to do with a preference for certain foods. As a team, we had decided not to intervene or try to get him to eat the school-recommended food. Herman liked certain foods, and, as long as he had something for lunch, the school professionals were all right with that. Foods and textures were not a battle that we wanted to address with Herman.

CRITICAL REFLECTIVE QUESTIONS

1. ASD is a very complex diagnosis, with considerations needing to be made, especially for communication. What connection does a student's lack of communication have to challenging behaviors? What did this look like for Herman?

2. Fine motor, gross motor, and tactile aversions or needs are often part of the sensory integration that students with autism need. What professionals should be consulted in determining these needs for Herman?

ACADEMIC LITERATURE CONNECTIONS

Hyatt, K., Stephenson, J., & Carter, M. (2009). A review of three controversial educational practices: Perceptual motor programs, sensory integration, and tinted lenses. *Education & Treatment of Children, 32*(2), 313–342.

Nungesser, N., & Watkins, R. (2005). Preschool teachers' perceptions and reactions to challenging classroom behavior: Implications for speech-language pathologist. *Language, Speech, and Hearing Services in Schools, 36*(2), 139–151.

7

BABBLING AND COOING

Infant Communication in the Body of a Kindergartener?

Amanda Zbacnik

This vignette explores the school situations of an individual with autism, a kindergarten girl named Beth. While potentially identified (because official diagnosis in the school setting does not occur until age seven) with autism, this case presents another very different look into the sensory and communication needs associated with autism. Specifically, Beth was prone to meltdowns and giving "snakebites" to those around her if deviation from her sensory integration schedule occurred.

VIGNETTE #7: BETH

Beth had autism, but it was so hard to understand how she was feeling. This was because the emotional expression on her face seemed to be consistent on a fairly consistent basis. Beth was a kindergartener who would babble and coo in a way very similar to an infant. Beth was a physically larger girl for a kindergartener. Her stature made her appear to be more like a second- or third-grader. Long story short, many people underestimated her physical and social capabilities based on her appearance.

Beth also had a preference for certain foods. Beth absolutely loved Goldfish crackers (which our speech-language pathologist capitalized on). The speech-language pathologist was fascinated by Beth in their speech sessions, where she showed her basic communication and American Sign Language signs over and over in the hope that Beth would choose to use some of the signs to communicate.

Ms. Brown would never forget the day, during snack time, when Beth finally communicated with the class. As a routine during our days, we had a snack and a drink, and on that day we were having Goldfish crackers and water. Snack time, though you wouldn't think it, was a bit challenging in that the adults needed to get around the table at an appropriate pace, making sure that some of the students (who had a hard time waiting) worked a little bit on developing patience but not so long as to cause a meltdown.

Knowing that Goldfish crackers were Beth's preferred snack, we would serve her first, hoping that she would communicate with us if she wanted more. Well, Beth absolutely made this communication connection! And this did not just include one sign (fish). Beth was able to tap her fingertips together, indicating "more"; make the squiggly sign for "fish"; and close this out by rubbing her hand in a circular motion on her cheek, indicating "please." She would quickly eat her fish and then repeat this sequence of words two more times. All the staff that worked with her were absolutely thrilled!

Beth also had very intense gross motor sensory needs. Ms. Brown and the paraprofessional that worked closely with Beth were prompted to refer to a chart displaying a variety of "sensory diet" items. We got to learn how to use an elastic blanket strategy to roll Beth up into, essentially, a tortilla to provide a "hug" feeling. As Ms. Brown recalled, this was the first time that everyone in the room actually saw Beth smile while tightly wrapped into a tortilla. She let out a big coo, followed by the biggest smile imaginable. This memory continues to warm Ms. Brown's heart.

Another need of Beth was to understand self-regulation. When frustrated, Beth had the tendency to run up to people, grab their arm, and give them a "snakebite" twist with a grimace on her face. Beth was very strong for a kindergarten student. Two of the professionals she worked with actually had bruises on their arms. This led to the team deciding on including more fine motor "squeeze" items throughout her day. Ms. Brown remembers working very closely with the occupational therapist to try out different chewie necklaces and other squeeze gel toys that provided just the right amount of input.

Ultimately, after many trials, we discovered that Beth needed a compression vest. This vest had the option of adding weights in the pockets that could be removed or added through a Velcro snap. This vest allowed Beth to focus and be present in the special and general education classrooms and to not engage in the challenging snakebite behavior.

CRITICAL REFLECTIVE QUESTIONS

1. Both Herman and Beth were receiving services under the autism category. Even though having the same diagnosis, autism can look vastly different from individual to individual. Why is this concept important for educators to consider in creating individualized education plans?

2. A qualifying characteristic of autism evaluations is significant challenges in communication. What were some of the ways that school staff encouraged Herman and Beth to communicate their needs?

ACADEMIC LITERATURE CONNECTIONS

Hart, J. & Whalon, K. (2013). Misbehavior or missed opportunity? Challenges in interpreting the behavior of young children with autism spectrum disorder. *Early Childhood Education Journal, 41*(4), 257–263.

Slade, N., Eisenhower, A., Carter, A., & Blacher, J. (2018). Satisfaction with individualized education programs among parents of young children with ASD. *Exceptional Children, 84*(3), 242–260.

III

Equity Issue: Aggressive Behaviors Unidentified in Mainstream Classrooms

8

IS IT POSSIBLE TO STRIVE FOR INCLUSION WHILE ACKNOWLEDGING SAFETY ISSUES?

Manu Sharma

This vignette provides a glimpse into a kindergarten student who was not officially diagnosed or identified with any learning or behavioral exceptionality yet demonstrated violent and aggressive behaviors in the classroom. The teacher struggles when thinking about the safety of all the other students and the emotional and social well-being of the student displaying these aggressive behaviors. This case is based on the kindergarten student's unsafe behavior and asks for the teacher, parent, and principal to collaborate in addressing the matter, but this is easier said than done.

VIGNETTE #8: DARREN

In Ontario, the new kindergarten program brought about many abrupt changes that parents, teachers, and other colleagues were not prepared for. By 2016, all kindergarten classrooms in the province were to follow an inquiry-based approach while maintaining social and emotional growth of students. The new features of the kindergarten classrooms were uncapped enrollment and a co-partnership between the early childhood educator (ECE) and the kindergarten teacher, with no extra budget for resources and no common time training and integration of students with special needs.

At Riverview Elementary School, Ms. Parks was assigned to teach a kindergarten class starting halfway through the year in January. Ms. Parks learned that prior to her arrival this class had three teachers, and each of them left that teaching position for various reasons. She was also told by other teachers that the parent community was frustrated by all these changes given that it was their children's first year in this institution. Ms. Parks knew she was going to have a challenging semester, but she was optimistic about providing a stable and engaging second term to all the students.

As Ms. Parks became acclimated to the new school, teachers, students, and parents, she developed a deeper understanding of how the school ran. Ms. Parks was concerned that the administrator did not allocate a separate budget for kindergarten resources given the large size of this class, which had thirty-two students, of which ten required individual education plans due to special needs. Ms. Parks held an opening after-school meeting with parents to talk about how to build resources for the classroom.

Many parents supported providing school supplies, used books, and used toys. Noticing the parents of students with special needs often did not attend these after-school meetings, yet required the most resources and assistance, Ms. Parks called each of these parents of the students. The response rate improved, and ideas for helping their child to succeed in a crowded, loud, and energetic classroom were shared.

One parent did not respond to any phone messages or written notes sent home. The student, Darren, had an older brother in grade five in the same school who was very well mannered and achieved high grades. Unlike his brother, Darren often struggled with inquiry-based learning and classroom social rules and behaviors.

During the first month of Ms. Parks's teaching, Darren made siren-like sounds throughout the read-aloud readings for no apparent reason, disrupting the class. During group time activities, he exhibited bullying-like behaviors. He would swear, push other kids, and take away objects that students were playing with just to upset them and laugh about it.

These behaviors and actions were shared with the principal, Darren's parents, and other teachers in the school with the hopes of getting support and strategies to help Darren. Unfortunately, the principal said, "You need to resolve this with the parents and on your own." The other teacher who was consulted was concerned about the safety of other students and told Ms. Parks to notify immediately the parents of the children being harmed by Darren. Following this advice, Ms. Parks did share incidences that happened between students to the parents, without naming the students, as she too felt that the parents of all parties had a right to know.

Darren's parents did not respond to Ms. Parks's letters and phone messages of concern about Darren. As another short-term solution, Ms. Parks spoke with Darren's older brother to find out what helped Darren stay calm and focused at home. The older brother said, "He is never disruptive at home." Confused by this new information about Darren, Ms. Parks decided to ask Darren's older brother to relay her request to meet with the parents.

Finally, during the third month of Ms. Parks's teaching at Riverview, she met Darren's father by chance when he was dropping off Darren in the morning. Ms. Parks took the opportunity to speak with him that morning. As she listened to Darren's father speak about the importance of discipline in a variety of forms, she grew worried about the welfare of Darren, but she politely thanked his father for his insights.

The father reassured Ms. Parks that he would address these disruptive behaviors tonight when Darren came home from school. The next day, Darren came to school and did not utter a word or engage with anyone in the classroom. Darren's withdrawal lasted for a week. As a result, Ms. Parks decided to call the school's social worker and Children's Aid Society and also informed the principal of what steps she had taken.

The following week Darren's disruptive behaviors returned with triple the intensity. Darren started the day with throwing blueberries on every kid's head and taking every activity bin and spilling its contents all over the floor, ripping posters and students' work off the wall, screaming and biting students, and creating a state of crisis in the classroom. Although Ms. Parks had a good rapport with Darren, she was not able to get him to calm down. The ECE, who was sixty-five years old, was terrified of Darren and had shared with Ms. Parks that she would have nothing to do with this student.

The ECE also shared that Darren had been kicking her shins and punching her in the stomach when she had attempted to help him in January. With all this information in mind and knowing the safety plan put into the IEP for Darren, Ms. Parks led an emergency evacuation of the classroom and had the ECE inform the principal of what was happening.

The principal came out into the hallway and shouted at Ms. Parks for being unable to manage her class and disturbing her day. As Ms. Parks led the students down the hall to the Rainbow Room, which was full of storage but was the only available space in the school, she heard the principal slam the door shut of Ms. Parks's classroom, and then she saw the principal physically carrying kicking, screaming, and biting Darren into her office. Ms. Parks was overwhelmed and on the verge of a mental breakdown, as she turned to look at thirty-one students in this small storage room waiting for her to do something.

CRITICAL REFLECTIVE QUESTIONS

1. Why was Ms. Parks about to have a mental breakdown?
2. Why did the principal react in the manner that she did?
3. What are the consequences of Darren's behaviors for the other students whom he attacked and those who were bystanders?
4. Giving the challenging context of this classroom community, how can the teacher and the ECE meet the academic, social, and emotional expectations of the new kindergarten program?
5. How would you develop Darren's social and emotional capacity given the lack of parent engagement and the safety issues of other participants in the classroom?

ACADEMIC LITERATURE CONNECTIONS

Brunsting, N. C., Sreckovic, M. A., & Lane, K. L. (2014). Special education teacher burnout: A synthesis of research from 1979 to 2013. *Education and Treatment of Children, 37*(4), 681–711.

Resources and support for school mental health in Wisconsin: http://dpi.wi.gov/sspw/mental-health

Wei, X., Wagner, M., Christiano, E. R., Shattuck, P., & Yu, J. W. (2014). Special education services received by students with autism spectrum disorders from preschool through high school. *Journal of Special Education, 48*(3), 167–179.

9

A PARENT'S REQUEST

Keeping a Secret from a Student and His Older Brother

Manu Sharma

This vignette draws attention to the strain on the early childhood educator and the kindergarten teacher relationship to support students with autism. When the safety and mental health of the adults in the kindergarten setting gets pushed to the limits, what is expected to happen? This case provides vivid insight into the stress and ethical dilemmas teachers and early childhood educators face when left with a student with very high needs and a lack of support from administrators in a demanding classroom environment.

VIGNETTE #9: ANTHONY

All Ontario public schools had to have implemented a full-day kindergarten program beginning in 2016. At Woodland Elementary School there were going to be six full-day English-speaking kindergarten classrooms and two full-day French-speaking senior kindergarten classrooms. This year, there was a new vice principal named Ms. Pear.

It was an exciting year for Ms. Barry to be working at Woodland Elementary School. She had taught kindergarten before and was excited to teach it again at another school. As usual, the last week of August was to be used to set up the classroom.

Ms. Barry went in every day to design the classroom space to be friendly and supportive of the new full-day kindergarten curriculum. The room that was given to her was very small with one bathroom stall. Knowing that there was not much of a budget to buy kindergarten classroom supplies to help create an inquiry-based learning model, Ms. Barry went to secondhand stores and to the Dollar Store to purchase much of the equipment for her classroom.

As she wanted to have some mentorship by other teachers for kindergarten teaching, Ms. Barry walked to the other end of the school where the other three kindergarten classes were located side by side. She noticed that the three kindergarten classes already had pictures of students up on the wall and distinct activity centers and that both the early childhood educator and the kindergarten teacher were working together to set up the classroom. Excited by this work done in partnership, Ms. Barry went to Ms. Pear to ask for a list of her students as well as information on her early childhood educator partner.

Ms. Pear provided a class list of thirty-three students and stated that the early childhood educator designated to Ms. Barry's classroom was yet to be determined, but whoever took on this role would most likely be temporary in this position. Worried about the lack of human and physical resources, Ms. Barry began to think about how to get her future students' parents involved in helping build the resources for the classroom.

Before long, it was the first day of school; Ms. Barry held up her classroom sign proudly and walked her students to the classroom. There were many tears shed by the students as they waved goodbye to their parents. In the middle of the classroom stood a young and timid-looking adult, Ms. Pang.

Ms. Barry found out that morning that Ms. Pang was the short-term early childhood educator for the kindergarten class. Ms. Barry and Ms. Pang tried to comfort the students and to have them sit in a circle on the alphabet carpet. The students took some time to adjust and get comfortable with one another. The first week was all about playing and socializing while maintaining a safe environment in the classroom.

There was one particular student who was quiet and kept to himself during playtime and socializing opportunities. This student was Anthony. After a quick phone call home, Ms. Barry learned that Anthony had been diagnosed with autism but his parents wanted to keep this a secret. Anthony had an older brother in the school named Michael and two twin younger brothers at home with his mother.

Autism manifested in different ways for Anthony; sometimes, he would be antisocial, but later, as he became comfortable in the school environment, he started demonstrating loud outbursts that terrified other students. Anthony would knock over bins in the kindergarten environment, scream like a siren constantly, run out of the classroom and out of the school, and kick both of the teachers.

These behaviors were challenging to Ms. Pear; her first question was what could be done in the classroom to support Anthony. Ms. Barry shared that Anthony had a visual schedule, he had support of the early childhood educator and the teacher as often as possible, and constant communication was being made with the parents at home. Moreover, Ms. Barry explained that she had brought Anthony up to the school support team and would like a safety plan in place in his IEP. Ms. Pear agreed but also suggested that next morning Ms. Barry should place a childproof lock on the door.

Ms. Barry was unhappy with this suggestion of a childproof lock, as she thought this would just make the other students more vulnerable to Anthony's loud outbursts. Ms. Barry did not believe that safety for one student should put the other thirty-two students in danger. She gave Ms. Pear examples of multiple students being hit in the head by objects that Anthony threw at them and Anthony spitting and kicking and pulling the hair of the other students. Ms. Pear was not interested in these anecdotes and suggested that to put a lock on the door is the best way possible to deal with the situation.

Ms. Pang had already told Ms. Barry that she would no longer be working with Anthony, as he had kicked her several times in the shin. Now, it was only Ms. Barry who had to accommodate Anthony while addressing the other thirty-two pairs of eyes that were looking at her. Ms. Barry would come to work every day exhausted, stressed, and nervous, afraid that Anthony's behaviors would keep escalating and that somebody would get hurt.

Meanwhile, Anthony's mother became very bossy and started to dictate and demand that Anthony be socialized with other students. She firmly believed her child was normal and could overcome his autism given support and attention. Ms. Barry was overwhelmed and did not know how to respond to this demanding parent, uninterested vice principal, and fearful early childhood educator.

On one Friday afternoon, after lunch break, Ms. Barry returned to her classroom. She noticed that all of the hard work that she had done with putting up posters and creating centers with material she bought or donated for the classwork and work done by her students was destroyed. She knew this was a result of Anthony's violent and loud outburst while she was at lunch. She looked at her classroom and teared up.

This was the third outburst this week. Ms. Barry was ready to take a mental leave of absence but was conflicted by her duty toward the other thirty-two children. The vice principal came into Ms. Barry's classroom to inform her that Ms. Pang had quit. Ms. Barry had a panic attack.

CRITICAL REFLECTIVE QUESTIONS

1. Should teachers be expected to keep special needs of students confidential when they conflict with the safety of other students?
2. How should Ms. Barry explain to the other parents the high number of accidents that students incurred due to Anthony's outbursts?
3. When would it be possible to start teaching content, such as reading and math skills, in a volatile kindergarten classroom space?
4. How can teachers address the lack of human and physical resources? Should teachers address them?
5. Why do you think Ms. Pear responded to Anthony's behavior in this manner?

ACADEMIC LITERATURE CONNECTIONS

Gibson, A., Pelletier, J., & Jackman, E. (2012). Can we work together? Preliminary findings from an examination of ECE and teacher dynamics in full-day early learning-kindergarten. *Unpublished manuscript. Ontario Institute for the Study of Education, University of Toronto, Toronto, Ontario, Canada.*

Stover, K., & Pelletier, J. (2018). Does full-day kindergarten reduce parenting daily hassles? *Canadian Journal of Education, 41*(1), 276–300.

10

DISTURBING BEHAVIOR INVADING ANOTHER STUDENT'S PRIVACY

Manu Sharma

This vignette examines an unexpected disturbing behavior displayed by a male kindergarten student toward a female kindergarten student in gym class. This behavior was shared with the homeroom kindergarten teacher, who was aware of the male kindergarten student's higher emotional risk-taking behavior, intellectual advancement, and physical stature in relation to the rest of his classmates but was not aware of inappropriate touching actions he had demonstrated in gym class.

This case highlights the sensitivity of explaining such disturbing behavior to a racialized parent who is in denial and hostile in response to the teacher. The teacher is left wondering how to support the female student who was violated and how to address the male student and his mother.

VIGNETTE #10: RAHUL

Ms. Apple was ready to begin teaching her enthusiastic kindergarten students at Willowdale Elementary School. It was already the middle of October, and the class was still learning to adjust to behavior expectations and creating a calm yet exploratory classroom setting. As in every kindergarten class, there were some students who came to school already knowing how to read and write the alphabet and were further along in their academic skills than students who were just beginning to acclimate to the school environment and socializing with others for the very first time.

One particularly bright student was Rahul. He was taller than the rest of this class and physically and emotionally resembled grade two students. Ms. Apple would often praise Rahul for his ability to finish work and help students who were struggling. However, despite the leadership opportunities and interesting tasks given to Rahul, he would instigate fights between students.

When speaking to Rahul, Ms. Apple would praise his academic ability and his strong command of the English language but also remind him that other students were still in the process of learning. Ms. Apple provided Rahul extra homework and more challenging activities in the classroom setting. Unfortunately, the praising and different challenging tasks did not offset the fighting that Rahul would engage in.

Concerned about Rahul's physical strength and academic progress, Ms. Apple approached the in-school support team, which included the vice principal and the principal. She recommended that Rahul be given a higher grade placement and perhaps be tested for gifted programs. While waiting to meet with the in-school support team, Ms. Apple observed that Rahul would often linger by the classroom window when the junior recess bell went off.

Rahul would ask to go outside and play with the junior grade students, but given that he was only in kindergarten, he was not allowed to leave the classroom setting. After a reminder of the kindergarten schedule was given to Rahul, he would kick the bookstand in frustration and swear back at the teacher.

After this incident, Ms. Apple called Rahul's mother and shared her thoughts about the gifted program and her concerns about the emotional outburst behavior that Rahul displayed. Rahul's mother, Michelle, was very pleased about the gifted program idea but quick to say that Rahul had often struggled with making friends his own age and had a very independent and stubborn personality.

Michelle shared that, even when Rahul went to the park in the summer, he would be hanging out with boys who were three or four years older than he and he would speak to them as though he was at the same level as they.

Moreover, Michelle said that these social interactions concerned her because the older boys at the park would call Rahul at home asking for him to come and play with them. Listening attentively, Ms. Apple reassured Michelle that the in-school support team would meet to discuss a plan for Rahul and that Michelle would be able to attend this meeting.

Unfortunately, in the course of the next two weeks there were several emotional outbursts and the use of profanity and physical violence displayed by Rahul in the kindergarten classroom. Rahul's behaviors became unsafe for other students. As a result, Ms. Apple shared this information with the school principal, and they collectively decided to put Rahul on a communication log that informed Rahul's mother about his social behavior.

At the end of these two weeks, Rahul had a huge temper tantrum in the classroom over one of the students wanting to play with him, and he started throwing objects on the floor and across the room. Rahul knew there would be consequences and that the incident would be shared in the communication booklet that had to be signed by his mother.

After Rahul had cooled down and Ms. Apple had led the students to the gymnasium for their gym class, Ms. Apple had decided to speak with Rahul in private. Leaving the classroom door open so that other teachers could look in, she spoke with Rahul about his behavior and the outburst. This led to Rahul quietly sobbing and saying that his mother hits him whenever he brings home a bad communication report.

Ms. Apple was very concerned learning this new fact; given the law to report child abuse, she had to file a report with Children's Aid Society. Ms. Apple allowed Rahul to go to the gym. During her preparation period, she disclosed what had been shared by Rahul with the school principal. The principal was in agreement for the course of action that Ms. Apple had taken. The principal rolled her eyes at the end and said, "I can't believe these troubled kids and their behaviors starting so violently as early as they do in kindergarten."

After the class had returned from the gym, the gym teacher asked to speak with Ms. Apple outside the classroom. The early childhood educator took over and read a short story to the students on the carpet while Ms. Apple and the gym teacher spoke out in the hallway. The gym teacher shared that Rahul had pushed Kelly, a girl who was the tiniest girl in the class, into the corner of the gym and tried to put his hand up her dress into her underwear.

The gym teacher said that he was aware Kelly did not speak a great deal of English but was in tears for most of the gym class. He also shared that he learned about this incident because a group of girls came to him and told him that Kelly was crying. And when the gym teacher tried to console Kelly, she pointed at Rahul and indicated what action he did.

As a result, the gym teacher was disgusted and wanted Ms. Apple to speak to his mother. Ms. Apple did not know how this new layer of challenges would be taken up by Michelle and the school principal. At the end of the school day, she wrote a long email to the principal, sharing what had happened in the gym class. Ms. Apple left the school feeling exhausted and stressed out. When she arrived the next morning, she was called to the principal's office. There were Rahul, his mother, and his aunt looking very tense. What was Ms. Apple to do now?

CRITICAL REFLECTIVE QUESTIONS

1. Should class assignments be based upon age groupings or ability? Why?
2. Given the context of a full-day kindergarten classroom and the twenty-nine other students, what is Ms. Apple's professional and ethical duty toward Rahul's educational experience?
3. Does gifted academic and social ability trump the behavioral outbursts and possible molestation of a peer?
4. How can a teacher keep an open mind and an open heart toward a student like Rahul when they feel exhausted and disgusted by what behaviors they see?

ACADEMIC LITERATURE CONNECTIONS

Elder, E. (2018). Student behaviour as workplace violence. *Education Law Journal*, *27*(2), 211–218.
Harklau, L., Lew, S., & Yang, A. (2018). Tracking and ability grouping in kindergarten to 12th grade settings. *The TESOL Encyclopedia of English Language Teaching*, 1–6.

11

NO ONE IS ACTIVELY LISTENING AND IT IS CREATING ACCIDENTS

Manu Sharma

This vignette describes the turmoil a beginning teacher feels when she sees a student in her nontraditional health classroom space conducting themselves in unsafe ways and brings it to the attention of the administrator, who does not address her concerns. Although many prewarnings were shared and many staff were aware of the situation, the administrator, who was busy, silently permitted the unsafe behavior to escalate to the point of causing physical pain for the grade two student and creating trauma for his classmates. The teacher is left to confront the administrator about the lack of responsiveness but then is put in a difficult situation where power and politics become the central issues, rather than the student's situation.

VIGNETTE #11: JACK

Ms. Lou, a first-year health and physical education teacher at Washington Elementary and Middle School, awaited her third period, a grades two and three split class. Ms. Lou had been trying to get this class to settle down for more than a month now. It was just around the Canadian Thanksgiving holiday, and the class still had new students joining that had not settled.

This particular class originally had twenty-five students, but by mid-October there were thirty-three students. The class enjoyed physical activity and demonstrated their enthusiasm by shouting and using loud noises. There were many students with strong personalities in this class that demanded a great deal of attention and energy from Ms. Lou.

Being a health and physical educator was a great deal of fun, but this subject also provided a great deal of risks of physical injury. The unstructured classroom environment, the open space of the gym, and sports equipment that was accessible during classes became the foundational ingredients of mayhem for this grades two and three split class. Ms. Lou was often worried about a particular grade two student whose name was Jack. He joined the class in late September and was full of energy.

Usually students were expected to sit in these four squads respectively when they enter the gym, but Jack always ran around the gym screaming. The other students in the class would watch Jack giggle, and sometimes other students would join him in running around the gym. Ms. Lou blew her whistle and asked them to sit down, but the students would not listen and Jack was their leader.

Worried about physical injury and classroom management, Ms. Lou contacted the homeroom teacher, Ms. Twinkle, for this grades two and three split class. When Ms. Lou told Ms. Twinkle about what happened in gym class, Ms. Twinkle was not surprised. Ms. Twinkle shared that Jack had a hard time focusing in the classroom setting and would also distract other students by making loud sounds and drawing attention to himself.

Recently, Jack had started to become physically violent with other students in the homeroom classroom. Ms. Twinkle said she had already tried to call Jack's parents and informed the other students not to engage in physical violence with Jack. Ms. Lou said that she had been asking Jack to take on leadership responsibilities by handing out equipment to get him refocused in the gym class, but he had taken this opportunity to throw things in his peers' faces.

Luckily, no one had been seriously injured. After this heartfelt conversation, Ms. Lou and Ms. Twinkle decided to ask the principal to request the school social worker to visit Jack during the school day.

In response to this request, the principal shared that Jack's parents had to approve the visitation of a social worker. If they did not, the school was not able to provide a social worker to Jack. As a result, Ms. Lou and Ms. Twinkle wrote a letter together requesting the permission of Jack's parents to allow for a social worker to help Jack with his unfocused energy and violence in the classrooms. Unfortunately, the letter came back with a response of no.

Being that it was just before the Thanksgiving holiday break, Ms. Lou decided to call Jack's parents at home and share her concerns one more time. Jack's parents said they appreciated the phone call but there was nothing wrong with their son. They said he just needed to be able to use his energy in classes in a productive manner. Ms. Lou shared the results of this phone call with the principal and Ms. Twinkle.

After the Thanksgiving break, Ms. Lou started the health portion of her class. She focused on nutritional foods and getting students to understand the difference between good touch and bad touch. Ms. Lou had only the girls' changing room as a classroom space to do this health lesson; the principal had told her this school was already full and all the rooms were being used. Given that there were hooks and benches and cubbies and a tighter space overall, Ms. Lou was concerned about Jack's ability to cope with this new setting.

Unfortunately, as she suspected, the first time she held a health class in the girls' changing room, Jack jumped from bench to bench and tried to hook himself onto a hook. Luckily, Ms. Lou had a student teacher who was there to observe how health content was to be taught, and she asked her to sit with Jack on a bench while the rest of the class sat on the floor listening to the health lesson. Given that the student teacher was new and was able to give 100 percent of her attention to Jack, this helped Jack calm down and allow for a class to take place.

Given this debacle, Ms. Lou decided to share what was happening in the health class setting with the principal and Ms. Twinkle, hoping that a new classroom space or an educational assistant could be attached to this particular class.

Unfortunately, both of these hopes were not answered. Ms. Lou was aware that the student teacher was not going to come to the next health class and that she would be by herself with all thirty-three students in this cramped space. She strongly advocated at the end of her discussion with the principal that something had to be done before Jack got physically hurt or hurt another child. Ms. Lou was adamant that this alternative space for the health class was not a safe environment because it did not have access to a phone and did not have any windows that allowed for other colleagues who walked in the hall of the basement of the school to see what was going on.

In response to these concerns, the principal offered a walkie-talkie from the office and told her to buzz her when something went wrong and mentioned to keep the changing room door open. Ms. Lou was not content with this solution, but given the power differences between the principal and her as a first-year teacher, she decided to follow suit.

The following week when the split grades two and three class came to have their second lesson in health, Ms. Lou noticed that Jack was drinking a pop can and held the change room door open for his classmates. As the classmates came into the change room, Jack held out his hand and aggressively high-fived each classmate.

Ms. Lou asked everyone to take a seat on the floor, and she allowed Jack to sit on the bench to give him some space while he finished his drink. Things started out okay. Ms. Lou was able to show pictures of the four Canadian food groups to the class, but then all of a sudden, Jack decided to start hopping benches again. Ms. Lou stopped her lesson and asked Jack to stop. She physically came toward him to help him come off the bench, but before Ms. Lou could get to Jack, he had jumped and missed the next bench. Jack had broken his two front teeth, and there was a pool of blood on the floor and all over his mouth and dripping onto his shirt.

Ms. Lou grabbed the walkie-talkie and asked for the principal to come and support the classroom given this huge accident. Ms. Lou was enraged because she felt this situation could have been prevented had the principal taken her concerns more seriously and provided her with better assistance.

The class was watching Jack in terror, and some started to cry. Ms. Lou looked at her watch and noticed five minutes had already gone by and the principal had not shown up. She communicated through the walkie-talkie to the office again; she was reassured by the school secretary that the principal had heard the message. Ms. Lou was a nervous wreck about what had happened in the change room. Ten minutes had gone by now, and still the principal had not appeared.

As a result, Ms. Lou sent two students as partners up to the office to ask for the principal to come downstairs to the basement and help with this situation. Seventeen minutes passed before the principal showed up with a coffee mug in her hand. Ms. Lou gave the principal a disgruntled look and said, "This is an emergency, and it would be nice if we all could care about our students a little more."

The principal responded, "Ms. Lou, I will see you in my office at the end of the day." The rest of the class was still crying and overwhelmed with fifteen minutes of the period left to go. Ms. Lou wondered what she should do to calm down the class. Then, all of a sudden another student shouted that he had found Jack's tooth and held it up. Ms. Lou was in shock and did not know how to respond.

CRITICAL REFLECTIVE QUESTIONS

1. Should parents have the ultimate decision in whether their child receives social work services in the school setting when other students are being put in a situation of danger and trauma?
2. Do you think that Ms. Lou did things in an ethical manner? Given her circumstances, would you do anything different?
3. How could Jack be supported beyond what Ms. Lou offered?
4. How do you explain (if at all) Jack's behavior and actions to the rest of the class?
5. Is Ms. Lou, the principal, or Ms. Twinkle responsible for the "trauma" released on other students in Jack's vicinity and on Jack? Why?

ACADEMIC LITERATURE CONNECTIONS

Committee on School Health. (2004). School-based mental health services. *Pediatrics*, *113*(6), 1839–1845.
Tuters, S., & Portelli, J. (2017). Ontario school principals and diversity: Are they prepared to lead for equity? *International Journal of Educational Management*, *31*(5), 598–611.

12

DIFFICULT TRANSITIONS

Entering and Exiting Classroom Environments

Manu Sharma

In this vignette, the teacher is challenged to work with a parent who is in denial of his kindergarten-aged son's learning and behavioral needs. The teacher struggles with gaining the full picture of Sunny's home life, as his mother was away for a good period of time and his father is not willing to share much. The teacher looks to the administrator for support, and the outcome is not favorable in providing a long-term solution that helps resolve the disruptive and selected mutism behavior that Sunny displays.

The case allows future teachers to think through how to work with a disruptive student who has difficulty with transitions and cooperating with other peers while working with their parent and administrator who may not be as helpful as they would appreciate.

VIGNETTE #12: SUNNY

Black Bear Elementary School is a small inner-city school situated in the northern part of Toronto. The school list included a wide range of racially diverse students; many students were first-generation immigrants. Ms. Valerie had set up her full-day kindergarten classroom with bright posters and happy images. Ms. Valerie expected to see twenty-nine students on the very first day of school. As usual, teachers gathered in the schoolyard with a sign indicating their classroom number, in hopes that parents and students could identify which class they belonged to.

As the bell rang, Ms. Valerie took her students to the magical classroom with the green shiny fabric on the door. Inside the classroom was Ms. Malka, who was setting up the morning snack for all of the incoming students. There were small juice boxes and apple slices in front of every seat at roundtables throughout the classroom. As the students were ushered in, there were many tears and frightful fears emerging from the little three- and four-year-olds.

Ms. Valerie and Ms. Malka decided to start the day with a short story and musical entertainment. Some students appreciated the music and started to dance, and some students listened to the short story with gorgeous pictures. As the week went on, Ms. Valerie and Ms. Malka tried to maintain a routine schedule to help all the students learn the consistency of their school day. As the teachers began to understand the needs of the various students in the classroom, they realized that patience and safety would be their main priority.

There were seven students in the classroom who did not speak English, two of whom were diagnosed with selective mutism. There were three students who had very strong behavioral concerns, especially when it came time to share toys and resources during center time. None of the students had been identified as having autism or attention deficit disorder. Ms. Valerie and Ms. Malka had a very hard time keeping the students engaged and feeling safe while they learned in this new school environment.

By the beginning of October, a new student, Sunny, had been assigned to Ms. Valerie and Ms. Malka's class. Sunny was a senior kindergarten student who had recently turned five years old. His parents were from China, and currently he was living with his dad. Sunny started off being a very quiet child in the classroom space as he observed all the things that were happening in the classroom.

By the end of the week, Sunny started to display strong anger toward students who wished to play with him during center time. Sunny would scream and hit his head on the floor when the students came near him. He would start destroying anything that was in his path. Both Ms. Valerie and Ms. Malka tried to calm him down, but it was very difficult, as Sunny did not want anything to do with anyone.

Worried about his behavioral response to other people's presence, Ms. Valerie and Ms. Malka spoke with Sunny's dad at the end of the day when he came to pick his son up. Sunny's dad shared that Sunny had never behaved like this before and he had been to a daycare since he was two years old. Sunny's dad also told the teachers that Sunny's mom had been in China for the last three years and was not around for Sunny as he was going through his formative years. However, she would be coming in early November back to Toronto.

The month of October was full of challenges with Sunny. His meltdowns and tantrums would get louder and more violent and frequent. There was a struggle every day to get Sunny to enter into the class, get ready to go out for recess, and prepare for home time. Sunny got into a routine of just sitting or lying flat on the floor in the hallway outside of the classroom.

These issues were regularly communicated with Sunny's dad, but he would often laugh them off, saying, "Don't worry; he's just being silly." Then, the father would leave the child in the hallway and go to work. The teachers were getting very concerned that Sunny was being neglected at home and that these behavioral emotions and actions were a response to not receiving enough attention.

The teachers had informed the administration about what was going on, but the principal had said Sunny was only acclimating to kindergarten in the school. Teachers were told not to worry about his outbursts at this point. As the wintry snow arrived in late October, Sunny did not want to wear his winter clothes and boots. He would throw his boots and winter clothing down the hallway and lie down on the floor.

One time, he hit another student from a different class with his boot, which flew through the air, as students were getting ready for recess, blackening the student's eye. As a result, Sunny was kept inside and asked to go to the principal's office to explain his actions. Although Sunny had limited English, he had enough to communicate how he felt and what he wanted. Sunny was sent back from the principal's office, shortly after recess, with an iPad. The teachers were baffled and did not understand why the consequence for Sunny's behavior was being given an iPad and how the iPad was to help him change his ways.

Ms. Valerie went to speak with the principal to find out the purpose of the iPad, and she was told this was a good distraction for Sunny. Further, it was communicated that he should have access to it during transitional times. Ms. Valerie decided to use the iPad as the principal had directed; however, this caused a great deal of jealousy and violence among other students in the classroom. Sunny became more aggressive as students tried to look over his shoulder and see what he was doing on the iPad.

It was on a Friday afternoon that Sunny stopped yelling in response to the students coming close to him while he was on the iPad; rather, he slapped the child right across his face, leaving a sweltering red mark of a handprint on his classmate's face.

Unfortunately, the transitional times to go home, go to recess, and enter into the classroom in the morning did not get easier with the iPad. Sunny always wanted to stay inside and not engage with others. Following this violent incident, there was serious concern for the safety of other students in the classroom. Ms. Valerie and Ms. Malka took Sunny to the principal's office and debriefed the principal as to what had happened recently.

The principal said she was very busy and did not have time to address the matter right now. "Please take Sunny back to your classroom." The teachers realized that there was not a lot of support from the administrator. The father also refused to acknowledge the violent and disruptive behaviors of his son.

The next week was the beginning of November, and Sunny's mother had arrived from China. Ms. Valerie and Ms. Malka thought this would be the solution to the problems that Sunny was displaying in the classroom. However, when the teachers met Sunny's mother and saw how she interacted with her son, it was evident that there was a lack of attachment. It seemed as though Sunny ignored his mother and did not respond to anything that she asked.

Sunny's mother asking for a hug from her son, which Sunny refused, further reinforced this observation. The teachers and Sunny's parents stood in silence, watching Sunny have another transitional meltdown in the middle of the hallway. It was now thirty minutes after the school bell had rung, and Sunny was not getting ready to go home.

CRITICAL REFLECTIVE QUESTIONS

1. What should Ms. Valerie do when Sunny is lying flat on the hallway floor and does not wish to come into the classroom? Meanwhile, the rest of the class is waiting for Ms. Valerie to start teaching the morning message.
2. How is the teacher to address concerns to a parent who refuses to acknowledge the behaviors of his child?
3. Principals can get very busy and then provide a short-term solution to a long-term problem. How effective is this strategy?
4. Why do you think Sunny behaved in this way?
5. What obligations do you as an educator have to the other students and their parents in the classroom given the sensitive issue of Sunny's meltdowns and violent behavior?

ACADEMIC LITERATURE CONNECTIONS

Cook, A., Spinazzola, J., Ford, J., Lanktree, C., Blaustein, M., Cloitre, M., . . . Mallah, K. (2017). Complex trauma in children and adolescents. *Psychiatric Annals, 35*(5), 390–398.

Rivard, M., Terroux, A., Parent-Boursier, C., & Mercier, C. (2014). Determinants of stress in parents of children with autism spectrum disorders. *Journal of Autism and Developmental Disorders, 44*(7), 1609–1620.

13

TEACHING PHYSICALLY AGGRESSIVE STUDENTS

How Much Support Does a School Provide?

Amanda Zbacnik

This vignette vividly shares aggressive behaviors of a kindergarten boy in the special and music education setting. It explores the challenges of making the least restrictive environment accessible to students exhibiting challenging behaviors, while considering the safety of other students/ staff.

VIGNETTE #13: JUSTIN

In this vignette, Ms. Brown provides some insight on a boy named Justin. It was December during her first year of teaching, and administration (principal and dean of students) called the special educator, Ms. Brown, into a meeting where she was told that a transfer student was coming into the special education resource room. Ms. Brown was a little surprised at this statement, seeing that it was December and the child was a kindergartener. Nonetheless, she was willing to work with him. In his IEP, Ms. Brown noted that Justin had some aggressive behaviors, but she did not fully understand what this might entail.

By mid-December, a week before the holiday break, Ms. Brown remembers sitting down in the special education classroom and hearing a knock on the door. Ms. Brown opened the door (where the dean of students, Justin, and Justin's parents stood), through which Justin came bursting into the room, ripping everything off the walls (posters, pencil sharpener, and books off the classroom library bookshelves) before running back out into the hallway.

It was as if a tornado had come in and out of the classroom. It was one of those moments that probably took longer than the actual occurrence seemed; Ms. Brown stood there, absolutely in shock. How on earth could she meet her other students' and Justin's needs, with so many intense behaviors present?

Ms. Brown immediately went down to the principal's office, where Justin was also sitting, trying to be calmed down by the secretary, principal, and his parents. Luckily, the dean of students had also witnessed the destruction that had just happened in the classroom. Knowing this information, the response was that interviews were going to be held that afternoon to hire a paraprofessional to help in redirecting Justin's aggressive behaviors. Ms. Brown thought this was a very good idea.

After the interviews were held (with very short notice), Justin's first paraprofessional was the mother of some of the music students that Ms. Brown had in the high school choir (this educator wore many different teaching hats in her first teaching job). The paraprofessional was a woman in her mid-fifties, and she possessed incredible amounts of patience.

However, as noted in Justin's previous IEP, he also liked to engage in physically pushing or hitting those around him. Even though having, seemingly, endless amounts of patience, this paraprofessional just could not cope with Justin's sprinting away or shoving of his general education peers, and she resigned after one week.

Ms. Brown recalls taking on the role of Justin's general education music teacher (part of the music education hat) and having to keep Justin a safe distance away from his peers due to the inability to pick up on the trigger of when he would, randomly, run up and push or shove a peer. This preferred seating arrangement worked during the singing portion of class but posed challenges during interactive circle songs.

During these songs, students were to hold hands and slowly move. Another challenging time was the lining up process at the end of class where Justin simply could not control his body. After Justin's original paraprofessional resigned, Ms. Brown remembers the new hire, a six-foot-two-inch male, coming to school wearing umpire gear.

You see, Justin's hitting/shoving was not solely focused on his classmates. The paraprofessionals were also receiving some of his blows. Justin's new paraprofessional was more effective at picking up on some of Justin's triggers and keeping other students safe. After two weeks of seeming harmony, the honeymoon period ended. Justin, while walking in the hallway, went approximately fifteen feet out of his way to push a little girl down to the ground.

As a result, it was decided by administration (because, ironically, this was witnessed in the hallway outside of the main office) that Justin needed a more restrictive learning environment to meet his needs and to protect the rights of innocent bystanders.

CRITICAL REFLECTIVE QUESTIONS

1. It is a known fact in the world of special education that students with special needs can be transferred into your classroom at any time during the school year (in my experience, even in the final five days of the school year). Consider the learning curve that must occur for the new student in getting used to a new school environment. What makes this particularly challenging when the student has previous data indicating displaying aggressive behaviors?

2. Hiring a paraprofessional that is a great fit (academically and behaviorally) for a student is critical to the student's success. What interview questions might the hiring committee have asked specific to Justin's needs?

3. Safety of all individuals in the school environment needs to happen at all times. Behavior plans should be in place with established plans when the student gets into crisis mode. What might some of Justin's behavior intervention plan steps include?

ACADEMIC LITERATURE CONNECTIONS

Fisher, M. & Ociepka, A. (2011). We're all in this together: Identifying meaningful outcomes for K–6 students of teacher candidates. *Teacher Education and Special Education, 34*(2), 152–175.

Killu, K. (2008). Developing effective behavior intervention plans: Suggestions for school personnel. *Intervention in School and Clinic, 43*(3), 140–149.

Langenkamp, A. (2016). Effects of school mobility on adolescent social ties and academic adjustment. *Youth & Society*, *48*(6), 810–833.

IV

Equity Issue: Religion

14

INEXPERIENCED TEACHER AND EXPERIENCED STUDENT DISCUSSING SEX EDUCATION

Manu Sharma

This vignette explores the vulnerability of a teacher's identity and how it can contrast with the life experiences of her middle school students. When a teacher's lack of knowledge and experience is evident and her discomfort is apparent, how should she address this with her students, if at all? In this case a grade eight student shares her lived experiences of an abortion and active sex life, which startles the teacher, who is not sure how to address these life experiences of the student.

VIGNETTE #14: MINDY

It was Miss Black's second year at Bayview Elementary and Middle School teaching health and physical education to students ranging from kindergarten to grade eight. Bayview was considered to be an urban school full of first-generation students from multiple cultural backgrounds and different religious affiliations.

Miss Black was a conservative teacher who practiced a faith that believed in engaging in sexual activity only after marriage. Miss Black was not married and still sorting out her personal life when it came to exploring sexual activity. Thus, when she was expected to teach the health curriculum on safe sex practices and alternatives to teenage pregnancy, her personal values and experiences were limited and clashed with the public curriculum for grade eight students. However, she was expected to deliver the curriculum.

It was almost the end of the school year, and Miss Black had held off on this particular health unit as much as possible. She had shared her uneasiness with one of her close colleagues in the school without revealing too many personal details because she believed in a strict divide between professional and personal life. Her colleague, Mary, suggested that she act confident and deliver the curriculum as if she knew about sexual activity and the consequences that students may face if they enter into it too early.

Mary was a good friend of Miss Black and reassured her that it was okay to teach this unit at the end of the year because it would prepare students to be more conscientious during the summer break. Miss Black felt a sigh of relief after sharing these thoughts with Mary.

Miss Black thought she would deliver this curriculum through a biological lens that allowed her to speak to the science component of sexual intercourse and what the consequences would be if a pregnancy did occur. Miss Black prepared diagrams and found a short video to illustrate the journey of the sperm meeting the egg and creating the essence of life.

Still uneasy with these preparations, Miss Black decided to consult with public health nurses of Canada to ensure she had the most educational video on educating young teenage girls on the impact of teenage pregnancy, exploring sexual activity, and safe sex practices.

One of the public health nurses offered to come in as a guest speaker for one of the classes and share safe sex practices and also conduct a conversation of what it means to engage in sexual activity with informed consent. Miss Black was very content with and appreciative of what the public nurse had offered. As a result, Miss Black booked the second health class in this unit for the public nurse to come in and speak.

The night before the first health class in this unit, Miss Black did not sleep a wink. Miss Black was anxious and fearful to find out how the students would react to all this content because it was still new to her. The next morning, the grade eight girls met Miss Black in the health classroom for their scheduled class before lunch. Miss Black began the lesson by saying that today she would cover only the biological reproductive organs of both males and females and explain their functions and different parts.

The grade eight girls giggled. Miss Black remained focused on delivering the lesson that she had so tightly planned about the biological components of each reproductive organ. She had handed out a worksheet for the students to follow along with and fill in the blanks, label the reproductive organs, and explain their functions. Most of the students did comply, but there were many students gossiping and talking throughout the lesson.

As a result, Miss Black decided to offer the class the opportunity to write down questions that they had on a piece of paper anonymously and put them in a cardboard box she had found in the classroom. The box was sent around the room. When it came back to Miss Black, she shared that she would look at the questions and share her thoughts in the next class.

Miss Black articulated that it was okay to feel uncomfortable, nervous, and shy about the content everyone was learning. And, out of nowhere, a student named Mindy raised her hand and said, "Miss Black, this is not new for us; we're not shy. We want to talk about how to feel more pleasure when engaging in sexual intercourse."

Miss Black did not know how to immediately respond to this, but then she remembered that the guest visit was scheduled for the next class with the nurse. As a result, Miss Black said that the public health nurse would discuss safe sex practices and help with answering Mindy's question. The bell rang, and Miss Black took a deep breath and sighed. This had been a very challenging class for her to deliver. Three days later, the second health class took place.

In preparation, the nurse and Miss Black had talked on the phone about the anonymous questions. The nurse arrived with eighteen bananas and condoms and a sunny disposition and jumped right in by answering the main themes of the anonymous questions. Most of the themes were about masturbation, sexual positions, and the dangers of sexually transmitted infections. The nurse applauded the girls for the honest questions. Then, she explained safe sex practices by handing out a banana and a condom to each student and teaching them how to put the condom on the banana without piercing the latex. The students were very engaged.

Miss Black walked around the room and assisted as best as she could and did not speak very much during this lesson. After this hands-on opportunity, the nurse shared safe methods for protection that girls could use on themselves, such as birth control pills, diaphragms, spermicide, and so on. She ended the class by sharing that girls should be aware of what happens when these safe methods for protection do not work and that Miss Black would pick up on this matter in the next class. Miss Black was caught off guard at first and then said, "Of course," and dismissed the class just as the bell rang. Miss Black thanked the nurse for coming in and helping answer students' inquiries.

Miss Black went home and started to research what young girls could do if they did become pregnant. She became very nervous because she was aware that many students had different religious values and some did not support abortion. As Miss Black collected information about abortion and women's rights, teenage pregnancy, single parenting, young couple parenting, and adoption possibilities, she felt very uncomfortable and thought to herself that she should just promote abstinence.

The following week, Miss Black walked into class with pamphlets based on all the information she had collected on what happens when contraception doesn't work and pregnancy begins. She arranged a jigsaw activity and had students work in small groups of three to examine the pamphlets and then join other groups to understand what the other pamphlets said. Miss Black decided for one of the groups she would sit in and share the concept of abstinence without documents with a sincere passion in her heart for the well-being of students.

After the students had completed the jigsaw, Miss Black reemphasized the importance of abstinence and the painful decision-making related to abortion. At the end of class, Mindy said to Miss Black, "Thanks for teaching us this material, but it would have been more useful a year ago when I first got pregnant and had to go through my first abortion alone." Miss Black was astonished and was not sure how she could comfort or respond to Mindy. Before she knew it, the next group of students were filling into the class desks and Mindy had left.

At the end of the day, Miss Black went home and thought about how could she help Mindy. What would she say to her the next time they met? Beyond these initial thoughts, Miss Black wondered if she was required to tell the principal about the matter and whether she should call home to Mindy's parents.

CRITICAL REFLECTIVE QUESTIONS

1. How would you as a teacher (like Miss Black) teach about un-known experiences or unshared values given the public school cur-riculum expectations?
2. How do you respond to students who have had different life experi-ences than you?
3. Should Miss Black have confided in Mary? At the end of the story, should Mary share what she learned with the principal and/or Mindy's parents?
4. Is a teacher justified in promoting abstinence when he or she is fearful of negative outcomes?
5. Do you think more intimate questions about exploring sexual activ-ity should be answered by the teacher or parents at home? What if the parents have restrictive religious views on sexual activity be-fore marriage?

ACADEMIC LITERATURE CONNECTIONS

Bialystok, L., & Wright, J. (2017). "Just Say No": Public dissent over sexuality education and the Canadian national imaginary. *Discourse: Studies in the Cultural Politics of Education*, 1–15.
Young, P. D. (2017). Examining competing claims in the dialogue over sex education in Ontario: Women, rights, and religion. *Religious Studies and Theology*, *36*(2), 123–138.

15

A TEACHER'S ENTHUSIASM FOR CELEBRATING TRADITIONS

Manu Sharma

This vignette focuses on a teacher's interest and passion leading his students' activities and learning. Though the grade four teacher deems Halloween to be a cultural celebration, a new student and her mother view it as a religious event. The mother does not wish to allow her daughter to participate in the celebrations of Halloween, despite the grade four teacher's attempts to explain how these activities were not religious and met academic learning goals. One further complication this case draws attention to is how is a teacher to respond to the interested new student when her mother is imposing these restrictions on participating in the class activities?

VIGNETTE #15: NADINE

It was two weeks before Halloween at River Lake Public Elementary School, and Mr. Smith, the grade four teacher, loved Halloween! Mr. Smith joyfully took on the responsibility for the Halloween school parade and ensured that all teachers in the school were aware about it. He had created a flyer detailing what costumes would be acceptable and the ones that would not, according to school district policies. Teachers generally appreciated Mr. Smith's enthusiasm about Halloween.

This year Mr. Smith had decided to add another component to the Halloween festivities, haunted Halloween classroom door competitions.

Each classroom was offered the opportunity to participate in the haunted Halloween classroom door competition. As a result, ten classrooms decided to participate in the competition, and all fourteen classrooms decided to participate in the Halloween parade. Mr. Smith was happy to hear that so many classrooms wanted to participate in the Halloween activities.

Currently in his grade four classroom, they were carving pumpkins into jack-o'-lanterns, writing scary Halloween stories, creating advertisements for new chocolates and candies, and creating graphs of what chocolates and candies their classmates most enjoyed. Thus, it was evident that Mr. Smith took Halloween very seriously, as he had integrated it fully into his curriculum.

During the four guidance periods leading up to Halloween, Mr. Smith would often talk about his favorite Halloween moments and costumes that he wore while growing up in Québec. The students in Mr. Smith's class enjoyed seeing their teacher so involved in planning fun activities and assignments to keep students engaged with school curriculum. Mr. Smith's students soon became known as the ambassadors of Halloween at River Lake Public.

With one week before Halloween, Mr. Smith was told he was going to have a new student join his class. Mr. Smith went into the main office to welcome the young student, Nadine, to the school and bring her to his classroom. Nadine was reserved and a quiet student. Mr. Smith tried to bring Nadine up to speed with all of the festivities around Halloween that were happening in the classroom.

Nadine just looked at him, puzzled, and said, "My family does not celebrate Halloween; we are proud Jehovah's Witnesses." Mr. Smith was shocked and said he would talk to Nadine at the end of the school day. In the meantime, Nadine was expected to participate in classroom assignments, even though they were themed with the Halloween spirit. Nadine was a good student and decided to comply.

As the school day came to an end, Mr. Smith and Nadine spoke about how her first day had gone. Nadine said it was interesting but she was afraid she would be in trouble when she got home and told her mother about what she had done in school. Mr. Smith reassured her not to worry and said that he would also call Nadine's mother and let her know that this was all harmless fun and a good way to get students learning the basic skills they were expected to learn in grade four. Nadine was nervous for Mr. Smith and quietly said, "My mother is very strict about her religion, and I am expected to follow it even though I don't like to."

Mr. Smith asked Nadine to explain what she did not like about her mother's religion. Nadine responded that she was unable to celebrate any of her birthdays or engage with any fun school activities. Mr. Smith said he was sorry to hear this and that he would try his best to convince Nadine's mom to let her participate in Halloween next week. Nadine was happy to hear that Mr. Smith was ready to talk with her mother; she hugged Mr. Smith and said, "Thank you so much; you don't know how much this means to me." Nadine left the school feeling happy about the prospect of participating in Halloween.

Mr. Smith called Nadine's mother, Rihanna. He started his conversation out with small talk about how Nadine's behavior was wonderful in class and she seems to be adjusting to the school culture. Rihanna was suspicious in her tone and asked what he meant by school culture.

Mr. Smith said she enjoys the company of many students in the class and she has gotten into doing classwork. Rihanna was happy to hear this. Next, Mr. Smith shared that the school was going to do a couple of activities related to Halloween next week and that Nadine had expressed a desire to participate in them but she also had informed him that her family's religious affiliation was Jehovah's Witness. There was silence on the phone.

Rihanna cleared her throat and said, "With all due respect, Mr. Smith, my daughter must observe her religious identity and carry out her religious duties. Halloween is not a celebration I want my daughter to be a part of." Mr. Smith explained that there was no religious undertone to Halloween; rather, it was just a fun cultural activity. Rihanna said that it does not matter whether Halloween is religious or not; the point is that Nadine cannot participate in Halloween events.

Frustrated, Mr. Smith said, "Do you think it's fair that you subject your daughter to your religious views when she wishes to be a part of her classroom community and not feel isolated because she is unable to participate in Halloween activities?" Rihanna said, "You have no right to speak to me in this way; I will be contacting your principal tomorrow. And, as far as I'm concerned, this phone conversation is over." As a result, there was dead silence on the phone followed by a long beep.

Mr. Smith was not sure whether he had crossed an unprofessional boundary given his love for Halloween activities and desire to respect

Nadine's wishes to participate in them, which were both in conflict with Rhianna's religious views and values.

The next day, sure enough, Nadine and Rihanna were sitting in the principal's office, and Mr. Smith was asked to attend a meeting while someone else covered his class. As Mr. Smith sat down, he felt a strong sense of unease and tension in the room. He was not sure what would come of this meeting and how he could support his student in the face of Rhianna's religious values.

CRITICAL REFLECTIVE QUESTIONS

1. Should parents' religious identities influence and affect their children's ability to participate in school activities?
2. If there is a conflict between a child and his or her parents' religious values, how does the teacher respond to this tension while still remaining professional? Did Mr. Smith act appropriately?
3. In public schools that are shaped by a Western influence of cultural activities, such as Halloween, Christmas, Valentine's Day, St. Patrick's Day, Mother's Day, Father's Day, and so on, should religious identities be considered when participating in such cultural activities?
4. How does the teacher ensure that a student feels included when he or she is not able to participate in the mainstream classroom activities? What alternatives could Mr. Smith give to Nadine?
5. What would happen if Mr. Smith went ahead with his planned Halloween activities and disregarded Rhianna's views? What if Mr. Smith had never called Nadine's mom and decided to keep it a secret and let Nadine participate in the class activities. Would this be ethical?

ACADEMIC LITERATURE CONNECTIONS

Boas, E. M. (2016). Education in disguise: Sanctioning sexuality in elementary school Halloween celebrations. *Sex Education*, *16*(1), 91–104.
Hillier, C. (2014). "But we're already doing it": Ontario teachers' responses to policies on religious inclusion and accommodation in public schools. *Alberta Journal of Educational Research*, *60*(1), 43–61.

V

Equity Issue: Socioeconomic Status

16

OVERSTEPPING PROFESSIONAL BOUNDARIES

Can a Teacher Be Too Generous?

Manu Sharma

This vignette presents the generosity of a well-intentioned grade five teacher in the context of an urban school. This case demonstrates how a teacher's worry about the nutritional health of one male grade five student becomes a personal project, resulting in the teacher packing lunches regularly for the student. Unfortunately, a dilemma appears when the mother, who is unaware of what the teacher is doing, is offended by his actions and, moreover, is not happy when her son suffers an allergic reaction to the food provided by the teacher. What can be done when the teacher has the best of intentions, but the parent does not want his help?

VIGNETTE #16: JOSEPH

Mr. Vine taught the grade five class at Black Forest Elementary School. The school was situated in a low socioeconomic status neighborhood. Many of the students who attended Black Forest struggled financially at home. The demographics of the community that surrounded Black Forest were made up of African Canadian, Chinese, Vietnamese, and West Indian people. Many of the students were first-generation students in Canada.

As Mr. Vine had been teaching at Black Forest for over three years now, he had become familiar with the daily struggles that his first-generation students experienced at home. He was conscientious about different family structures, lack of food and home security, and lack of warm clothing during the winter season. Mr. Vine had become supportive of students with these daily challenges by providing extra snacks and used clothes that were clean for students when they needed them. This year Mr. Vine had a new student, named Joseph, who was a quiet and reserved person.

Mr. Vine read Joseph's student record and learned that he had been moving between schools for the past couple of years due to a custody battle that was rather aggressive. Joseph now lived with his mother and was one of her five sons. In the interest of trying to get to know Joseph, Mr. Vine asked Joseph to stay for fifteen minutes into the lunch break on the first Friday of the school year to have a conversation about how he is liking school and class and the new neighborhood. Joseph remained in the classroom as all of his classmates left for lunch.

Mr. Vine asked Joseph to go grab lunch and come sit with him at the roundtable in the classroom. Joseph quietly stood up, went into his locker, and returned with a small bag of chips. Mr. Vine felt disturbed that Joseph had such a small lunch, and, given his small stature, he was afraid that Joseph was malnourished. Mr. Vine offered some extra snacks that he had in his desk for students in the class, and Joseph politely declined. Although Mr. Vine was quite disturbed by Joseph's lack of lunch and quiet demeanor, he went on to ask about Joseph's siblings and what they all did for fun together.

Joseph shared that he had four brothers, all of them were older. Unfortunately, two of them had been recently arrested for jaywalking in the new neighborhood. Listening to Joseph and watching his body language and facial expression change into a vulnerable and sad state turned Mr. Vine's stomach into knots. Mr. Vine said he was sorry to hear about Joseph's two brothers being arrested, and then he tried to change the subject to what were some of the hobbies that Joseph liked to do.

Joseph, still very introspective, said that he did not have time for hobbies, as he had to help out with his two younger brothers when he got home from school. Joseph said his younger brothers needed help with their homework and needed to be fed dinner, so he has now taken to cooking quick and cheap meals. Mr. Vine asked, given that Joseph had to cook, did he enjoy cooking? Joseph proudly smiled and said he knew how to cook macaroni and cheese ten different ways. Mr. Vine was delighted to see Joseph smile; he promised that there would be some cooking projects that they would do together in the grade five classroom.

All of a sudden, the first lunch bell rang, and fifteen minutes had become thirty minutes. Thus, Mr. Vine told Joseph to go outside and play for the last fifteen minutes before classes began for the afternoon. Joseph politely picked up his small bag of chips that he had finished eating and threw it out in the classroom garbage can, thanked Mr. Vine for the conversation, and headed out to the playground area. Mr. Vine, overwhelmed by Joseph's maturity given the difficult situation he was in, felt he needed to do something more for Joseph.

The next day, Mr. Vine said to Joseph that he would bring him a nutritious lunch every day and that every Thursday they could have a conversation to check in about Joseph's adjustment to the new neighborhood, school, and life in general. Joseph was astonished to hear about this generous offer from Mr. Vine and said thank you kindly. Mr. Vine was delighted with this new opportunity to help support Joseph.

Unfortunately, other students in Mr. Vine's class heard about this arrangement and were not thrilled that Joseph got special attention from Mr. Vine. As a result, sometimes, students would say, "Hey, Mr. Vine, where is my lunch?" and "I wouldn't mind your cooking." Mr. Vine would just chuckle and say that is enough now and then continue on with his daily routine.

By the fourth Thursday, Joseph started opening up to Mr. Vine and telling him about all the different places he had lived and attended school; things were going well. However, later that afternoon, Joseph broke out in hives all over his body. Mr. Vine was not sure what had happened; his first thought was it was an allergic reaction to the food.

Based on school protocol, Mr. Vine called the school nurse, and she recommended that Joseph be taken to the nearest emergency hospital. So an ambulance was called. Mr. Vine also left a message for Joseph's mother, who was at work according to the voice greeting. Mr. Vine had to continue teaching the rest of the afternoon and was worried sick about Joseph, so he decided to drive up to the hospital at the end of the school day.

Mr. Vine found out that no one had come to get Joseph and that he was still in the waiting area but now asleep on a hospital bed. Mr. Vine had become emotionally attached to Joseph and cared for him like a son. Deep in his own thoughts, Mr. Vine took a seat beside Joseph's hospital bed. About an hour later, one of Joseph's brothers came to the hospital to take care of him. It looked like an older brother had been released from jail. Mr. Vine introduced himself and told the brother about what had happened. The older brother thanked Mr. Vine for his kindness and said he could go home.

Mr. Vine left the hospital feeling better that Joseph's older brother was taking care of Joseph. The next day Joseph did not come to school. There was a voice message left for him by Joseph's mother saying that she needed to talk with him, and just as Mr. Vine was leaving the office, the school principal said let's talk during the lunch break about Joseph because Joseph's mother had had a lengthy conversation with him that morning.

Mr. Vine took a deep breath and was not sure what to expect and walked with a heavy heart to his classroom. He started to have doubts about whether he had overstepped the boundaries of being a caring teacher, whether Joseph's mother potentially wanted to sue him, and whether the principal was going to reprimand his acts of kindness.

CRITICAL REFLECTIVE QUESTIONS

1. What is the boundary of a caring teacher and overstepping that line? Where does Mr. Vine fit with respect to your understanding of boundaries?
2. How can teachers bond with students they feel empathetic toward? If the student was not a victim of systematic poverty but of mental health issues, would the relationship between a caring teacher and the student look different?
3. Why does jaywalking most likely result in being arrested in low socioeconomic status neighborhoods and not in affluent neighborhoods?
4. Poverty plagues many students' lives. How can teachers address this in a meaningful way in their classroom?
5. How can parents play a role in assisting the educational experience of their child when they are struggling with poverty and its implications on their own lives?

ACADEMIC LITERATURE CONNECTIONS

Gollnick, D., & Chinn, P. (2017). Class and social economic status. In *Multicultural education in a pluralistic society* (10th ed., pp. 57–82). New York, NY: Pearson.

Lee, A. (Producer). (2016, September 13). *Pull yourself up by your bootstraps* [Audio podcast]. Retrieved from https://www.backstoryradio.org/blog/pull-yourself-up-by-your-bootstraps/

MacLeod, J. (2009). Social reproduction in theoretical perspective. In *Ain't no makin' it: Aspirations and attainment in a low-income neighborhood.* (3rd ed., pp. 11–24). New York, NY: Routledge.

Sokolower, J. (2014). Schools and the new Jim Crow: An interview with Michelle Alexander. In W. Au (ed.), *Rethinking multicultural education: Teaching for racial and cultural justice* (pp. 57–65). New York: Rethinking Schools Ltd.

17

THE CHALLENGE WITH LOCATING HIGH-INTEREST CURRICULUM FOR STUDENTS AT LOW READING LEVELS

Amanda Zbacnik

This vignette is focused on a tenth-grader in the special education classroom, with a passionate interest in choir. Imagine the challenge of locating age-appropriate curriculum for a high school student who reads at an elementary school level. These situations also make educators realize the extreme challenges that come from expecting an individual with a disability to live independently, when completing activities of daily living are of concern.

VIGNETTE #17: FAYE

During Ms. Brown's first year as a special educator, she worked with a student named Faye. In this K–12 school, Ms. Brown was currently providing special education service time to three elementary-aged students and then was assigned a sophomore student named Faye. Faye's previous case manager in the school had too many students on her caseload, so she was transferred to Ms. Brown.

Faye struggled in the area of reading comprehension, and, though a tenth-grader, she read at a second-grade level. As you can imagine, this made access to the curriculum in her high school content areas very difficult. Ms. Brown had to create the entire curriculum from scratch; it took a lot of brainstorming to come up with a modified curriculum that aligned with what Faye was learning in biology and health. Luckily, during Ms. Brown's time as a consultant for autism spectrum disorder, another educator had introduced her to Remedia publications, which is well known for having adaptive curriculum in many content areas.

In addition, Ms. Brown was responsible for providing Faye with a resource English course. So Ms. Brown also relied on Remedia publications and ordered some high interest and low readability reading curricula.

This made Ms. Brown aware of the challenge in working with individuals who are older and read at a very low level. Obviously, Ms. Brown never wanted Faye to feel like she was reading "babyish" materials. Ms. Brown remembers reading with Faye about celebrities. She was so excited to be reading about movie stars, musicians, and famous sports athletes. Her initial attitude was of disgust over having to be in a classroom with much younger students. But after catching her interest, Faye was excited to come to the English resource period and read.

Another major difference between a tenth- and a third-grader applies to attendance and truancy policies. During the first year as a teacher, Ms. Brown found herself faced with having to make the decision to call social services. At the end of February, Faye came to school for two weeks with a nonstop cough and had a look of exhaustion on her face. Faye disclosed that her house had not had heat for two weeks (and Minnesota has some very cold weather in February), and as a result Faye did not come to school for a week.

It was at that point that Ms. Brown made the call to social services (she tried calling Faye's landline number first, but it had been disconnected). The information was relayed to Ms. Brown that Faye's mother had just recently lost her job and was now working extra hours at the community's only gas station. This lack of parental supervision was causing Faye to not wake up on time for school and she was missing the bus. Not knowing what to do, Faye was simply walking around town, bumming cigarettes.

This is where Ms. Brown's appreciation and relationship with the school family liaison developed. On days that Faye missed the bus, the school family liaison would pick up Faye and bring her to school. This situation was eye opening as to the importance of parental involvement, for all children, but especially for those with disabilities. Just because Faye was sixteen, it did not mean that she was able to get herself up, dressed, fed, and out the door (this did become part of her transition goals shortly after this incident).

It is important that students find something that makes them want to come to school. For Faye, Ms. Brown was able to establish additional rapport with her through choir. Being part of a high school choir allowed Faye to socialize with same-aged peers and contribute toward a common goal. Every student needs to feel like they belong to something.

CRITICAL REFLECTIVE QUESTIONS

1. It is very common to be an elementary, middle, or high school special educator (and to work with multiple grade levels of students within these settings). What, however, are some of the challenges faced when serving students with special needs in a K–12 school?
2. Many schools, nationwide, have a compulsory attendance age of sixteen, which is when a student can drop out of school with parental permission. Why is this an issue for all students but especially for students with special needs?
3. What was the title of the person who helped Faye get to school? What other individuals, do you believe, were also involved in this process?

ACADEMIC LITERATURE CONNECTIONS

Christle, C., Jolivette, K., & Nelson, M. (2007). School characteristics related to high school dropout rates. *Remedial and Special Education, 28*(6), 325–339.

Kearney, C., & Kenkel, M. (2003). Bridging the gap among professionals who address youths with school absenteeism: Overview and suggestions for consensus. *Professional Psychology: Research and Practice, 34*(1), 57–65.

Ramrathan, L., & Ngubane, T. (2013). Instructional leadership in multi-grade classrooms: What can mono-grade teachers learn from their resilience? *Education as Change, 17*(1), 93–105.

18

DEATH OF A STUDENT'S MOTHER

How Much Should an Educator Get Involved?

Amanda Zbacnik

This vignette follows Brent, a high school student in the special education classroom, through events occurring during his tenth- and eleventh-grade years. It highlights the importance of placing a student with an educator that they trust to improve their reading, and not to be snarky with regard to children with low literacy skills. It also demonstrates how a student's investment in making attendance at school a priority can also gain the support of parent(s). Last, this vignette documents a special educator's visit to Brent's home, under dire circumstances.

VIGNETTE #18: BRENT

Brent didn't start out in Ms. Brown's resource room. Initially, he came to her from another special education case manager, an educator that was more likely to take students with specific learning disabilities. Ms. Brown was known to have the majority of students with intellectual disabilities on her caseload. Since Brent was a tenth-grader reading at a second-grade level, he was transferred to her classroom.

Brent's story is one of absolute resilience. He lived with his mom, who displayed an uninvolved parenting style. When Brent was born and identified as having a specific learning disability, his father made the decision to be completely out of Brent's life. Since Brent did not like riding the bus to school, he would wake up on his own and ride his bike two miles to school, to arrive at the same time (rain or shine). His previous case manager categorized Brent as a shy student, with temper control issues.

Ms. Brown, however, witnessed the self-regulation issues only once in her classroom. Brent enjoyed the weekly cooking class. The paraprofessional that was working with his group this particular week had not allowed Brent to make his green eggs and ham in the microwave. This angered Brent so much. To this day Ms. Brown can still see Brent's upset face calling this paraprofessional out on all of the injustices of not letting him complete his meal. The professionals in the resource room who had a good relationship with Brent were able to calm him down before it led to any more vulgarities.

At the end of Brent's junior year, he was up for reevaluation to identify a continuing need for special education services. His mother had not shown up for the previous year's IEP meeting, but, for a reevaluation, it was critical that she be part of the reporting process about where Brent was academically. After two phone call attempts, it took a handwritten note sent home with Brent to gain her attendance. This note said that, in order to continue your son's services in special education, her presence was required at the meeting. This reevaluation/IEP meeting was held at 7:30 on a Tuesday morning.

Ms. Brown remembers Brent's mother coming to the classroom door. She was ghostly white, thin as a rail, and smelled of alcohol. However, making sure that her son continued to receive services was important enough for her to come to the school. That moment mattered so much to Ms. Brown, as an educator. Ms. Brown felt that, to Brent's mother, it meant that her son enjoyed and found purpose in participating in the school environment.

What followed a month later was the most devastating situation that Ms. Brown had ever had to deal with as an educator. It actually made her question why certain children face and go through traumatic situations in the different home environments that they live in. For the first time in a year and a half, Brent didn't show up at his set place and time for two days in a row.

Brent would occasionally be ill, but this typically involved one day at home, after which he was ready to be back with his friends. After two days of absence, Ms. Brown was beginning to feel a little anxious. In these moments a teacher begins to trust their educator's intuition, that something wasn't quite right. After school, at the end of Brent's second day being gone, the assistant principal showed up at the classroom door requesting to talk with Ms. Brown.

Principal Lille mentioned that Brent was at home with his mother, who was very ill and may have been terminal. Brent's mother had been drinking so much alcohol that her liver was failing and skin was turning yellow from being poisoned by the alcohol. In that moment, Ms. Brown remembers her brain jumping in a thousand directions and wondering what could be done to help Brent.

Ms. Brown knew Brent's situation. She knew that his mother was the only one in the world that he cared about and she, him. Ms. Brown also knew that Brent would probably be hungry (as he had previously mentioned that there wasn't a lot of food in the house) and knew that he liked McDonald's.

So after school that day Ms. Brown went to McDonald's, picked up Brent's favorite double cheeseburger, fries, and a Coke and went to his home. After knocking on the door, it was opened by a chaplain. Ms. Brown introduced herself and mentioned that she just wanted to see how Brent was doing.

After the introduction, the chaplain told Ms. Brown that Brent's mother had just died. Ms. Brown was absolutely in shock and stood at the entrance of Brent's house, watching as he walked down the steps. He was shaking uncontrollably, and his face looked as white as a ghost. All Ms. Brown could say was "I'm so sorry, Brent." Ms. Brown gave him a hug, gave him his meal, got into her car, and burst into tears. As emotionally draining as this situation was, the most inspiring aspect of this was that Brent showed up to school the next day. School was a safe place for him. School was where he knew people loved him.

There is still a sense of unrest and some questions about whether Brent had some of his basic needs met, following the death of his mother. Since Brent was not yet eighteen, social workers got involved to find an appropriate placement for him. This involved Brent moving in with his grandparents who lived in a community thirty miles away. Ms. Brown was very sad about this decision, as she knew that Brent's grandparents lived in a rundown cabin, with occasional limited access to running water.

This was one situation that was completely out of the school professionals' control, and Ms. Brown had to say goodbye to Brent. The special educator knew that, after his junior year, he would be transferring to a different school district to finish out his high school career.

On a more positive note, the summer following Brent's junior year, Ms. Brown got the opportunity to see him at a county fair. Brent took a lot of pride in being the parking attendant for this event, and he loved his small town fair. To this day, Ms. Brown loves seeing previous students out and about in the community, getting involved at all different degrees. For some students with special needs, transition means joining a transition organization; others make the decision to live at home or work part time. It is important for individuals to stay active in order to find their purpose in life.

CRITICAL REFLECTIVE QUESTIONS

1. Parental involvement and communication are absolutely essential in the special education process. What strategies were used to get Brent's mother to attend meetings? If knowing that a parent is going through some extreme hardships in their personal lives, should educators recommend resources? If so, which ones are applicable to this case study?
2. The death of a parent is considered an adverse childhood experience. What sort of services would you recommend for Brent at his new school? Is placement with another family member the best option?
3. When a teacher's student experiences trauma, the teacher also feels emotional stress. What strategies are recommended to avoid teacher burnout?

ACADEMIC LITERATURE CONNECTIONS

Bethell, C., Solloway, M., Guinosso, S., Hissink, S., Srivastav, A., Ford, D., & Simpson, L. (2017). Prioritizing possibilities for child and family health: An agenda to address adverse childhood experiences and foster the social and emotional roots of well-being in pediatrics. *Academic Pediatrics, 17*(7), 36–50.
Fore, C., Martin, C., & Bender, W. (2002). Teacher burnout in special education: The causes and the recommended solutions. *High School Journal, 86*(1), 36–44.
Staples, K., & Diliberto, J. (2010). Guidelines for successful parent involvement: Working with parents of students with disabilities. *TEACHING Exceptional Children, 42*(6), 58–63.

19

EIGHTEEN AND A RUNAWAY
Refusal to Let Stepdad Collect
Social Security Disability Money

Amanda Zbacnik

When a student runs away from home and is an adult, there is a balancing act between what can and cannot be disclosed to parents. This vignette follows a twelfth-grade student, Connie, through her choices to become independent and have access to resources available to homeless students. The safety of school personnel over aggressive retaliation from parents is also discussed.

VIGNETTE #19: CONNIE

In special education, no one can ever underestimate the time of year when a student might be placed in your classroom. This was the case for Connie. She came to Ms. Brown's high school special education classroom during the last week of school, during her tenth-grade year. In a previous meeting with the school counselor, Ms. Brown was informed that Connie traveled to Minnesota from Missouri, had been at countless schools over the past three years, and had run away with her twin sisters and mother from an abusive family dynamic.

Ms. Brown was told via a restraining order document that Connie's stepfather had verbally and physically injured her mother, even to the extent of burning her mother with cigarettes on the arm and breasts. Even with these documented injuries, her mother decided to move back in with their stepfather.

Connie had an amazing start to her junior year. Things seemed to be going well academically, with work on transition skills, social connections, and physical health. Then, at the end of November, the Friday after Thanksgiving, Ms. Brown received a text message from another special educator at her school. The message was that Connie's family apartment had burned down and that a team of educators would be getting together before school on Monday to supply the family with essential food, clothing, and hygiene items.

Ms. Brown remembered feeling her heart drop in her chest and then going to the local news feed about this incident. Sure enough, there was Connie on the news telling the news anchor how her apartment and personal items went up in flames. Connie's family had been put up in a local hotel for two evenings, paid by the local community, until other housing arrangements could be made.

After getting home from her parents' on that Saturday, Ms. Brown made a big pan of lasagna and went to the hotel to give it to the family. At the front desk, Connie was definitely frazzled about the situation. Ms. Brown gave her a hug and the lasagna and asked her if there was anything else she needed at the moment. She said, "Thanks" for the lasagna and, "No, we pretty much have what we need right now." In the timeline of events, the loss of their apartment was a foreboding of instability to come.

At the beginning of Connie's senior year, her attendance at school was limited. She would be gone nine days in a row, often showing up for the first hour of the school day, and then take the transit bus downtown. Connie was very wise, however, about always showing up on the tenth day of the absence cycle in order to not get dropped and be considered truant. At the end of September, Connie turned eighteen, at which time she was able to sign her own IEP. She took a lot of pride in being a legal adult, although her attendance continued to be sporadic.

One Monday midmorning, Connie's mother called and asked if Ms. Brown knew where Connie was. Connie had not shown up to school that day, and her mom told Ms. Brown that Connie had made the decision to run away from home. Connie had gotten into a verbal fight with her stepdad over her Social Security disability money. She told him that she was going to a place where her family wouldn't be able to steal her money. Connie wanted to use the money to invest in herself.

This was one of the most challenging predicaments that Ms. Brown had ever faced. Since Connie was eighteen years old, she was able to access adult services but had not yet graduated from high school. The school counselor told Ms. Brown that Connie was finding refuge in an organization that supports homeless youth. Since Connie was eighteen, Ms. Brown was unable to pass this information onto Connie's mother. The privacy of Connie's placement had to be upheld, despite her mother's pleas to tell her where Connie was. The only thing Ms. Brown could say was that "Yes, I know where she is, and, yes, she is safe."

Connie was deemed homeless, so special transportation was arranged to pick her up from this homeless organization every day. Ms. Brown also took a special trip down to this organization to see Connie and make sure that her needs were being met in terms of food, clothing, and housing.

When Connie did come back to school, about once out of every ten days, Ms. Brown would ask how she was doing and take Connie, with the principal's permission, to the lost and found to make sure she had an ample supply of clothing. Connie did not graduate with her classmates from the high school. Instead, the homeless organization she was working with had arranged for her to receive instruction to get her GED. Although it pained school staff to not see her graduate with a high school diploma, they were happy that Connie was completing her education, though through an alternative route.

While keeping Connie's location private, Connie's father, a very large man known for previous aggressive behavior and a restraining order, marched up to the school. His body language was such that Ms. Brown immediately called the principal to intervene. The principal met him at the school's main entrance and ushered him into the office. Ms. Brown was called down to consult about the situation regarding his stepdaughter running away from home.

As she was eighteen there was nothing any educators could do but restate that Connie was safe, but school professionals could not tell him where she was located. This sent the stepfather into a fit of rage.

He started calling school professionals racists and demanding that we let him know where his stepdaughter was. The principal said, "Perhaps you want to apply to have a social worker get Connie the support she needs." This suggestion made by the principal quieted him down a lot, as Ms. Brown suspected that a social worker would have been the last person he wanted around his house. To this day, school professionals don't know where Connie ended up in life.

CRITICAL REFLECTIVE QUESTIONS

1. Students in special education transfer schools at higher rates than students without disabilities. What are some of the major challenges associated with this? Are there any benefits of a transfer?
2. Having a family experience a traumatic event, like Connie's apartment fire, has emotional impacts. What physical items was the school able to provide Connie's family with? What could be done to address the emotional stress?
3. One out of every fifty children are homeless. Based on Connie's story and the legal duties mentioned in the McKinney-Vento Homeless Assistance Act of 1987, what considerations need to be made in assisting these children?

ACADEMIC LITERATURE CONNECTIONS

Pervanidou, P., Agorastos, A., Kolaitis, G., & Chrousos, G. (2017). Neuroendocrine responses to early life stress and trauma and susceptibility to disease. *European Journal of Psychotraumatology, 8*(4).

Portwood, S., Shears, J., Nelson, E., & Thomas, L. (2015). Examining the impact of family services on homeless children. *Child & Family Social Work, 20*(4), 480–493.

Zehr, M. (2011). Student mobility, "many challenges arise in educating students who change schools frequently." *Education Week, 30*(15), 5.

VI

Equity Issue: Ethnicity

20

WHY DID THE TEACHER NOT RESPECT MY PEOPLE'S HISTORY?

Manu Sharma

This vignette presents the dilemma a special education teacher confronts when the history teacher is not aware of the indigenous background of a grade five student. The special education teacher is conflicted about the insensitivity and lack of awareness the history teacher has toward this student and his ethnic identity. This case then examines the tension that can arise between teachers when their rapport with students is different and affects the learning journey of that student.

VIGNETTE #20: KENNY

It was mid-November in Beacon Elementary School, a busy time of year. Besides Beacon Elementary School, there were two other adjacent schools, namely, an indigenous school and an inner city high school. Beacon was made up of many diverse immigrants with different socioeconomic status. The school had a climate of welcoming students and embracing their ethnic and socioeconomic identities and provided special education programs to support the different level of student abilities. Ms. Peacock ran one of the special education programs, the Home School Program for elementary students from grades three to five.

In the Home School Program, Ms. Peacock was busy preparing individual lessons for her six students. It is important to note that Ms. Peacock was a halftime teacher and taught only in the mornings. Her students would be integrated in regular mainstream classes for the afternoons.

Given the range of age groups and abilities, Ms. Peacock worked hard to establish a special rapport with each student and build an educational plan that met their interests and needs. Many students needed support with reading, writing, and basic math. Ms. Peacock was a friendly teacher who made herself available over the lunch hour to her students, just in case they wanted to talk. The homeschool class was made up of four girls and two boys.

Ms. Peacock tried to create a collaborative and safe learning environment for all six of her students. She provided many team-building games and activities to engage the students with one another. She also used a buddy system to help students learn from one another. In other words, she would have the older students help the younger students once the older students had completed their work. Most of the students appreciated these collaborative opportunities and became friends with one another.

However, there was one grade five student named Kenny, who chose not to collaborate or engage with other students in class. Kenny would sit at his desk looking sad, tired, and lost in thoughts. He would not finish his classwork and did not seem to respond to shiny stickers, good grades, or developing friendships. Ms. Peacock worried about his social and emotional well-being.

In the beginning of the school year, Kenny did participate in some reading activities. However, over the past two months, his participation decreased, and he maintained a gloomy disposition in the classroom. Ms. Peacock shared her concerns with Kenny's parents over the phone several times, but they reassured her that Kenny was okay.

The parents shared that Kenny had to participate in their indigenous traditions, which are often performed late at night. Ms. Peacock inquired where these indigenous traditions took place. The parents responded that they would drive up to a reservation where their ancestors once lived. Appreciating this new information, Ms. Peacock decided that she would ask any follow-up questions directly to Kenny. Ms. Peacock said thank you to Kenny's parents and politely hung up the phone.

Later on in the week, Ms. Peacock approached Kenny and reassured him that it was okay to be tired given that he was taken to so many indigenous traditional events, which required long drives of five hours or more. Kenny looked up at Ms. Peacock shocked that she knew what he had been up to with his parents. Kenny asked Ms. Peacock how she knew he was tired. Ms. Peacock shared that she spoke with Kenny's parents because she was worried about him always being so tired.

Kenny nodded his head and then said, "Well, I'm also supposed to take care of my baby sister as these traditional events take place." Ms. Peacock asked how old his baby sister was. Kenny said she was one and a half years old. Ms. Peacock was thrilled that Kenny was speaking to her, as this was a great deal of improvement from the past two months.

Ms. Peacock asked Kenny what some of the indigenous traditions were that Kenny and his family participated in. Kenny shared that he learned about oral traditions and rituals that were important to share to maintain indigenous knowledge. Ms. Peacock gently asked him if he knew the history of indigenous people in Canada.

All of a sudden Kenny's body language turned inward, and a sense of silence overtook him. Kenny would not make eye contact with Ms. Peacock. Afraid that she had said something wrong, Ms. Peacock touched base with Ms. Lydia, who taught Kenny in the afternoon. Lo and behold, Ms. Lydia shared that she had begun teaching about the indigenous history in Canada.

Unfortunately, she did not go into the deep details of the mistreatment of several indigenous people and the cultural genocide they faced. When Ms. Peacock shared that Kenny had been participating recently in oral traditions and rituals of the indigenous people because of his indigenous identity, Ms. Lydia looked surprised.

Ms. Lydia shared that she did not know that Kenny had an indigenous identity. Moreover, she did not know if she could talk about the cultural genocide of indigenous people given the fact that the students in her class were very young. Ms. Peacock pointed out that Kenny seemed to already know about what had happened to his ancestors, through his travels to the reservation with his parents.

Ms. Peacock mentioned that perhaps the sadness and gloomy disposition of Kenny in her classroom had to do with the lack of his indigenous identity being respected and taught about in truthful ways. Ms. Lydia was surprised by Ms. Peacock's insights on Kenny and indigenous history. Her response was defensive in nature.

Ms. Lydia stated that Ms. Peacock had no business telling her how to teach indigenous history and culture to her grade five class. Moreover, Ms. Lydia said Ms. Peacock's interference could be taken to the school board union. As Ms. Lydia's temperament became angry, Ms. Peacock began to become silent. Ms. Peacock had wanted to help her student Kenny and was not trying to critique Ms. Lydia, but, clearly, this was not the message Ms. Lydia received.

CRITICAL REFLECTIVE QUESTIONS

1. What should Ms. Peacock do in the particular moment and perhaps in the long term to support her student?
2. Do you think that Ms. Lydia had a right to be upset with Ms. Peacock's insights? Why?
3. How can the controversial topic of indigenous histories be taught to grade five students? Should it be taught?
4. If there was no indigenous student in Ms. Lydia's class, should indigenous history be taught and how?
5. Did the teachers know enough about indigenous history to meet the means of respecting Kenny's identity? If yes, how did they know enough? If no, what could be done?

ACADEMIC LITERATURE CONNECTIONS

Brown, D., & Wicken W. (2018, April 30). Interpreting the treaties: Historical agreements between the Crown and First Nations are fraught with ambiguity. Retrieved from https://www.canadashistory.ca/explore/politics-law/interpreting-the-treaties?utm_source=Canada%27s+History+Newsletter&utm_campaign=8a0b45d165-EMAIL_CAMPAIGN_2018_05_02&utm_medium=email&utm_term=0_8145df6f6e-8a0b45d165-284533113

Dunbar-Ortiz, R., Gilio-Whitaker, D., & Press, B. (2016). *"All the real Indians died off": And 20 other myths about Native Americans*. Boston, MA: Beacon Press.

Treuer, A. (2012). *Everything you wanted to know about Indians but were afraid to ask*. Borealis Books.

Two Row Times. Retrieved from https://tworowtimes.com/

VII

Equity Issue: Language

21

SKILLS STUDENTS NEED

Helping Students Find a Voice

Amanda Zbacnik

This vignette draws attention to the importance of communication in the life of a child. The following is a case based on a second grade student's experience in the special and general education environment. It demonstrates how essential a means to communicate is to success in all areas of an individual's life (academic, social, emotional, and beyond).

VIGNETTE #21: TENLEY

When thinking of Tenley, Ms. Brown pictures the first student with special needs that she had the privilege to work with. Tenley was an eight-year-old African American girl with a slightly devious smile that could light up any room. Tenley was categorized as having multiple disabilities. She had a significant intellectual disability and was hard of hearing in both ears. Tenley also had some physical limitations in regard to fine and gross motor skills.

Due to Tenley being hard of hearing, Ms. Brown was introduced to the video series *Signing Times* with movie characters named Leah and Alex. It was in these twenty-minute sessions, which Tenley absolutely loved, where she learned basic sign language for farm animals, duties around the house, and play items and how to finger spell.

When working with Tenley, initially, she was the only student on Ms. Brown's special education caseload. The classroom consisted of just Tenley and Ms. Brown. There were very few resources to begin with, so Ms. Brown found herself looking for a lot of online resources related to the alphabet, numbers, and other functional skills that could be used on a daily basis. Daily lessons with Tenley were three hours in length, with the other 50 percent of Ms. Brown's teaching load including the teaching of the entire K–12 instrumental and choral music program.

Interestingly enough, Ms. Brown had the opportunity to connect with Tenley in the special education environment and as a music educator in the second-grade classroom. Tenley absolutely loved being around her peers. Since Tenley had some communication issues, she could share her agreement or disagreement about her peers' conversations only through grunts and some sign language. It was tough for her peers to understand and interact with Tenley.

It wasn't until the December of Ms. Brown's first year working with Tenley that the IEP team made the decision to start looking into some alternative communication devices for her. The first devices for developing communication were not expensive or fancy by any means. The purchase order included a basic Go Talker with Board Maker symbols that were cut and pasted into a grid. After the manual assembly was completed, the sheets were slid into the electronic device. From there, Tenley was able to see how to respond via the pictures on her board.

The Go Talker was a step up for interaction because previously all she had was a picture exchange communication system (PECS), which she did not actually carry. The paraprofessional always went with her to the general education classroom, art, physical education, and music specialists. Being that an adult had always held the PECS, you can only imagine how excited Tenley was to hold this device. She had her voice back!

CRITICAL REFLECTIVE QUESTIONS

1. What were some of Tenley's strengths?
2. What were some of the activities of daily living that were affected by Tenley's disability?

3. What process should an IEP team go through when selecting an assistive technology device for a student with communication needs?

ACADEMIC LITERATURE CONNECTIONS

Buzaid, A., Dodge, M., Handmacher, L., & Kiltz, P. (2013). Activities of daily living: Evaluation and treatment in persons with multiple sclerosis. *Physical Medicine and Rehabilitation Clinics of North America, 24*(4), 629–638.

Farmer, J., Allsopp, D., & Ferron, J. (2015). Impact of the personal strengths program on self-determination of college students with LD and/or ADHD. *Learning Disability Quarterly, 38*(3), 145–159.

Springer, R. (2009). Speech in an emergency. *Speech Technology, 14*(3), 42.

22

WHAT "CARROT" DRIVES YOUR STUDENTS?

Amanda Zbacnik

This vignette continues to explore the routines of second-grader Tenley and how important the use of incentives can be for motivating and making transitions easier in the classroom environment. Physical challenges during adaptive physical education and recess are explored. Lastly, misconceptions about IEP team members conclude this case study.

VIGNETTE #22: TENLEY CONTINUED

One of the wonderful things Ms. Brown recalls about Tenley includes her fascination with SpongeBob SquarePants. She absolutely loved anything to do with this cartoon character. Ms. Brown remembers the adaptive physical education teacher coming to work with Tenley. One of her major goals was to work on balance and doing stretches to assist her in developing a normal looking walking gait.

On one particular Friday morning, the developmental adapted physical education teacher brought some SpongeBob step-up cups. Essentially, these were the same cups that had been brought to previous sessions (without the SpongeBob stickers on them) and were thrown across the gymnasium. Tenley needed to step on top of the cups, working on her balance, and then hold onto the connected ropes with her hands. Then, the task was to walk around the gymnasium while balancing on the cups and holding the ropes. When previously asked to do this, it equated to disaster.

However, things changed when the SpongeBob stickers were included. Ms. Brown will never forget the smile that came across her face when trying out her SpongeBob cups. She was practically speed walking around the gymnasium! Tenley's brilliant white smile still stays in Ms. Brown's memory to this day.

Also, in relation to physical exercise, Tenley absolutely loved recess. However, the transition from the playground back into the school was extremely challenging. Ms. Brown clearly recalled Tenley's paraprofessional coming to her and stating, "She refuses to come in." (Tenley had been left under the supervision of the playground aide so the paraprofessional could communicate this to me.) So the IEP team had to try many things to help improve this transition.

One of the major strategies included having a visual timer, where Tenley removed little red dots for every ten minutes of recess time from a chart. This worked a majority of the time. However, there was also a phase where Tenley would simply refuse and lay out in the snow until the principal was called to come and assist in the situation.

You can imagine Ms. Brown's surprise as a new special educator when for the first time the paraprofessional came back to the special education classroom without Tenley. The message was relayed that the principal was trying to coax Tenley back into the building. So Ms. Brown bundled up in her winter gear and went outside to help.

Under the direction of the principal, it was decided that a fireman's carry could be used to get the student safely back inside. During the winter, having Tenley ride in a sled back to the school steps was also effective. However, the most effective strategy was to pair Tenley up with a student in her second-grade general education class. This buddy would walk her back to the special education room, where both would be rewarded with a star sticker upon showing up. Taking the adults out of the picture and allowing for peer interaction simplified the transition from recess back to school.

Another very vivid memory that involved the first exposure to working with parents/guardians of students with special needs involved the principal providing Ms. Brown with the following information about Tenley's mother: "Mom is very knowledgeable, has a master's degree, and works at a community college in the field of education." Ms. Brown wasn't sure why his statement made her blood pressure spike so much in that moment (because this young mother happened to be just about the best person any teacher could want to work with).

However, Ms. Brown remembers having so many socioeconomic and racial stereotypes shattered in her mind upon interacting with Tenley's mother at the first IEP meeting. Being that Tenley was an African American little girl, you can imagine Ms. Brown's surprise when mom was Caucasian. You can imagine even more surprise on Ms. Brown's part when Mom was the only parent at the IEP meeting. She mentioned that Tenley's father was no longer in the picture. This meeting was a gentle reminder that parents/guardians come in all shapes, sizes, colors, and genders.

CRITICAL REFLECTIVE QUESTIONS

1. What role did student interest play in getting Tenley motivated to work toward her goals?
2. Transitions can be a very challenging part of classroom management. What strategies were tried to transition Tenley from recess back to the classroom? Ultimately, what was most effective?
3. Special education teachers and parents/guardians need to work together collaboratively in order to help the student successfully achieve their IEP/transition goals. Why is it so important for educators to not have preconceived notions about what a "traditional" family unit may look like?

ACADEMIC LITERATURE CONNECTIONS

Banerjee, R., & Horn, E. (2013). Supporting classroom transitions between daily routines: Strategies and tips. *Young Exceptional Children, 16*(2), 3–14.

Nayir, F. (2017). The relationship between student motivation and class engagement levels. *Eurasian Journal of Educational Research, 71*, 59–77.

23

STUDENT REFUSALS TO COMPLETE TASKS

A Communication Challenge or
Statement of Strong Will?

Amanda Zbacnik

This vignette highlights the need to make considerations that benefit the student holistically. The second-grade girl, Nicole, is presented with academic, communication, social, and physical challenges in which many IEP team members, including the speech-language pathologist and school nurse, need to make tough decisions on Nicole's behalf. Lice anyone?

VIGNETTE #23: NICOLE

When Ms. Brown thought of Nicole, she pictured a big smile—the biggest smile you can imagine for this little girl of Native American descent. Nicole remained in the general education classroom for kindergarten and first grade and had gotten through just fine. But due to complications at birth, she was diagnosed with aphasia, from lack of oxygen during the birthing process. While this definitely had an effect on Nicole's communication skills, she was very bright intellectually. The major barrier for her was expressing to others the knowledge that she possessed.

Nicole absolutely loved being around her twin sister. However, their interaction was often laced with struggle because her twin sister often felt embarrassed by her sister's high-pitched squeals, grunts, and refusals in her communication. Furthermore, Nicole had a bit of a stubborn streak (this Ms. Brown actually really admired because, once agreeing to complete a task, she was persistent and determined to complete it to the greatest extreme possible).

On the other extreme of the spectrum, her stubbornness often led to Nicole refusing to do some academic tasks and, in terms of adaptive physical education, refusing to do the physical activities that were requested of her. At this point, the staff that worked with Nicole were not sure of the reason behind the refusals because she did not have a means for communicating her logic.

Ms. Brown was very fortunate that, at this second school, there was an exceptional speech-language pathologist. She was willing to teach all of the students in the class basic sign language to help them communicate with the teacher and the paraprofessionals that also worked with them. In Nicole's case, because she was intellectually able to decipher from a large variety of symbols, the process to select an augmentative communication device began.

Initially, Nicole was so excited to use the Dynavox in order to talk with her peers. She would practice using it during story time and circle time and at stations with her classmates. The Dynavox, however, was quite heavy, with a strap that secured around the neck and over the shoulder for easy transport. This device might have been ideal for an individual with more limited mobility, but, for a very active eight-year-old girl, carrying a five-pound device around was challenging and a bit annoying.

At this point, Nicole began making the decision to simply leave her communication device outside on the playground, in the cafeteria, or in the hallway. Obviously, this became a bit of a concern for the special education staff due to the fact that this piece of equipment cost $1,200.

Educators need to make the assistive technology meet the needs of the student. It did not matter that the communication device was user friendly and easy to navigate. It did not meet Nicole's needs for mobility, leading to frustration over not being able to engage in soccer and other gross motor activities without feeling weighed down.

Another story worth sharing about Nicole involves the school nurse and an epidemic of lice that went through the elementary school. The school procedure was that, if a student had any live lice on their head, they had to immediately be sent home. So, when Nicole's twin sister was

discovered to have lice, after the nurse did a check in the general education classroom, she came to check on the students in Ms. Brown's special
education resource room.

Sure enough, Nicole had head lice, so her mom had to come and pick
up both of the girls and take them home. After that, the paraprofessionals
in Ms. Brown's room rampantly began cleaning stuffed animals and all
surfaces that had been touched by Nicole. The nurse had a talk with their
mom on the procedures for getting rid of lice in the home environment,
and the mother agreed to follow through with these steps. The twins came
back to school two days later; the nurse checked their heads, and they still
had head lice. Obviously, the nurse had to call Mom and send the girls
home again. This same scenario happened another time.

Upon the last check, the nurse called upon the Native American school
liaison, who had some connections with services on the reservation. This
liaison was able to contact a cleaning service, which entered Nicole's
home and cleaned everything top to bottom. Lice scares are not fun!

CRITICAL REFLECTIVE QUESTIONS

1. Refusal to complete a task (physical or academic) was the most
   challenging behavior exhibited by Nicole. What ideas or classroom
   management strategies do you have to ensure students are not engaging in this behavior?
2. During the process to locate an augmentative communication device for Nicole, the SETT (student, environment, tasks, and tools)
   framework was followed. It was believed, by the IEP team, that the
   tool provided was capable of accomplishing the tasks for the student. However, there were issues with the environment section of
   this process (arrangement—instructional and physical; support—
   available to both the student and the staff; materials and equipment—commonly used by others in the environment; access issues—technological, physical, and instructional; and attitudes and
   expectations—staff, family, and others). What barriers did Nicole
   face that made her decide not to use her Dynavox?
3. Concerning the head lice, the school was lucky to have a Native
   American school liaison that recommended a cleaning service for

the students' home. What, as an educator, can you do to deal with lice in the classroom? What can you recommend for parents?

ACADEMIC LITERATURE CONNECTIONS

Bailey, R., Parette, H., Stoner, J., Angell, M., & Carroll, K. (2006). Family members' perceptions of augmentative and alternative communication device use. *Language, Speech, and Hearing Services in Schools, 37*(1), 50–60.

Bright, K., Boone, S., & Gerba, C. (2010). Occurrence of bacteria and viruses on elementary classroom surfaces and the potential role of classroom hygiene in the spread of infectious diseases. *Journal of School Nursing, 26*(1), 33–41.

Lane, K., Capizzi, A., Fisher, M., & Ennis, R. (2012). Secondary prevention efforts at the middle school level: An application of the behavior education program. *Education & Treatment of Children, 35*(1), 51–90.

VIII

Equity Issue: Difference in Parental Mindsets

24

THE POWER OF SELF-FULFILLING PROPHECY

Amanda Zbacnik

This vignette examines some of the stigma associated with students leaving the general education classroom to receive reading instruction in the special education classroom. It also demonstrates the power that words have, particularly when coming from influential adults, on the academic expectations of students with special needs.

VIGNETTE #24: JOHNNY

Johnny was a wonderful kid. He was kind, loved to be around his peers, was physically active, and had a specific learning disability. His specific challenges were in the area of reading comprehension. Ms. Brown remembers Johnny being so willing to help others. Oftentimes, his body language suggested embarrassment, presumably over having to come to the special education room. In this moment, the stigma associated with special education came to the surface.

It was like he was a different student in the general education classroom versus the special education resource room. Johnny (as observed to complete the most up-to-date and accurate reevaluation) was extremely social in the general education classroom versus a more withdrawn personality in the special education environment.

The moment that Ms. Brown met Johnny's parents made her think about self-fulfilling prophecy and how a parent's perception of how they performed academically in school can have positive or devastating effects on a child. When Ms. Brown sat down at the IEP meeting with Johnny's parents, she talked about the struggles that their son was having with reading comprehension. Specifically, this involved recalling main events, telling the names of major characters, and where the story was taking place.

Ms. Brown will never forget the response that she got: "Well, we're just happy that Johnny's in school. Neither of us was ever good at reading either." Johnny was sitting right next to his dad as those words came out of his mouth. Ms. Brown thinks about that moment and how, even as a third-grader, parental influence (either positive or negative) can shape a child's academic journey through their kindergarten to senior year experience.

CRITICAL REFLECTIVE QUESTIONS

1. Consider the least restrictive environment for a student like Johnny. In your opinion, was pulling him out of the general education classroom to receive reading instruction in the special education resource room the best option? If not, what other interventions/ strategies could have been tried?
2. For at least a decade, research has been done connecting mindset with achievement. If students believe they can learn a given subject, even a hard one, they stick with it longer and do better than if they believe they are "just bad at it." For Johnny, the challenges related to his ability to read may stem from things deeper than just his beliefs. What kind of conversation might a special educator need to have with parents who justify their child's performance (academically or behaviorally) based on their past school experiences?

ACADEMIC LITERATURE CONNECTIONS

Grace, D., & Brandt, M. (2006). Ready for success in kindergarten: A comparative analysis of teacher, parent, and administrator beliefs in Hawaii. *Journal of Early Childhood Research*, *4*(3), 223–258.

Marx, T., Hart, J., Nelson, L., Love, J., Baxter, C., Gartin, B., & Schaefer Whitby, P. (2014). Guiding IEP teams on meeting the least restrictive environment mandate. *Intervention in School and Clinic, 50*(1), 45–50.

25

MEALS OF SWEETS AND SODA

Can Educators Intervene in the Personal Health Choices of Their Students?

Amanda Zbacnik

This vignette focuses on parental influence on the vulnerable life decisions of a kindergarten boy. Denny, under the direction of his parents, begins to think that certain actions are healthy and normal forms of recreation. In fact, these choices in the long term would be detrimental to Denny's overall health.

VIGNETTE #25: DENNY

Denny came to Ms. Brown's class as a kindergartener; at the time, he weighed 125 pounds. His diet at home consisted of drinking soda with every meal and eating as many sweets as his parents could supply off the shelves from the Dollar Store. As a result, one of Denny's IEP goals was to improve his nutrition.

Another noticeable thing about Denny was that practically all of his baby teeth had been rotted down. This was the aftermath of being fed or consuming juice or soda and sugary items in the early stages of his life. More positively, however, Denny was such an enjoyable student. He loved school and the school staff that worked with him. Day after day, his toothless grin could make anyone smile.

Denny was a prime example of how the home environment plays an immense part in a student's understanding of what healthy choices are available. Both of Denny's parents also engaged in drinking soda with every meal and consumed sugary items. Both were, by American standards, obese. As part of Ms. Brown's programming, her classroom received a grant to go on weekly bowling outings.

Ms. Brown wanted to find a way to provide the students in the classroom with some healthy recreational activities that they could enjoy for their entire lives. Denny absolutely loved our Wednesday afternoon bowling outings and was very physically capable of rolling the ball down the alley without any assistance.

The most concerning experience related to Denny involved his at-home choice of a weekend recreational activity with his parents. One Monday morning, Ms. Brown asked what each student had done over the weekend. Denny replied, "I went on a walk with my parents," to which Ms. Brown responded, "Oh, that sounds really fun." She should have stopped there. Then, Ms. Brown asked him where he went and what he did on the walk.

Denny replied that he walked around town with his parents to find the stubs of cigarette butts. His and his sister's job was to place the remaining cigarette butts in a coffee can for their parents. Once at home, the parents engaged in smoking the remains of the cigarette butts. This situation was most influential in making Ms. Brown think about what children view as "normal." In Denny's mind, this situation was a child–parent time quality activity.

CRITICAL REFLECTIVE QUESTIONS

1. For many students in special education, who are cognitively vulnerable, what role should teachers take on in promoting a healthy lifestyle at school and in the home?
2. At what age should the dangers of smoking be introduced to students?
3. What, if anything, should be communicated with Denny's parents about what impact the behaviors he observes at home have on his well-being?

ACADEMIC LITERATURE CONNECTIONS

Mylnyk, B., Jacobson, D., Kelly, S., Belyea, M., Shaibi, G., Small, L., . . . Flavio, F. (2013). Promoting healthy lifestyles in high school adolescents: A randomized controlled trial. *American Journal of Preventive Medicine, 45*(4), 407–415.

Taylor, J., Taylor, A., Lewis, S., McNeill, A., Britton, J., Jones, L., . . . Bains, M. (2016). A qualitative evaluation of a novel intervention using insight into tobacco industry tactics to prevent the uptake of smoking in school-aged children. *BMC Public Health, 16*(1).

26

ENABLING OF STUDENTS WITH DISABILITIES

Are Some Parents' Actions Detrimental to Their Child?

Amanda Zbacnik

This vignette focuses on differences among academic and behavioral expectations of parents compared to school personnel. Brenda, a tenth-grader in the special education classroom, struggles to follow through with her capabilities in the school environment when much less is expected of her at home.

VIGNETTE #26: BRENDA

Brenda had an intellectual disability, which accentuated the fact that her parents did not allow her to be as independent as she could have been. Brenda had excellent handwriting and a very kind, caring demeanor in working with younger students. She really enjoyed her work experience at the elementary library and reading and singing with the kindergarten students. She also had a special connection to choir and enjoyed being part of the group.

There were also times that team members would request she complete tasks that were less than desirable to Brenda, and she would absolutely not have anything to do with this. Ms. Brown remembers an instance where she was refusing to do any classroom work. The adults in the room tried to use phrases like "We need to do this first; once completed you can have some free choice time." Per her IEP, allowing her time to write in her journal, listen to Jonas Brothers' music, or draw were all acceptable options after work completion.

Nothing seemed to work. After two days of refusals, the principal was consulted and asked to view this for himself. After he tried to coax her to complete some simple work, followed by refusal, he simply requested that she sit in Ms. Brown's chair that had wheels on it, and then he wheeled her down to her next class.

Brenda's parents were some of the most challenging parents that Ms. Brown ever had to work with, especially related to transition planning. It seemed Brenda was more capable of doing things than her parents believed. This created a tricky situation between home and school with regard to expectations. Whereas Brenda was definitely at a point where she should be able to shower by herself, she would come to school and say, "I wish my dad would just let me shower by myself."

From Ms. Brown's perspective, on behalf of a sixteen-year-old girl, this statement came across as a bit eccentric, in terms of the touching of physical anatomy. She was highly capable of doing this herself! However, Ms. Brown had to come to the conclusion that there will be some parents who hear the word "disability" and they perceive their child to be capable of less. It was Ms. Brown's hope that her fellow educators know that this is a falsehood.

From Ms. Brown's perspective, Brenda would have been highly capable of holding some sort of cleaning job or a job stocking library shelves. However, Brenda's parents decided that she required an aide in a transition program and that she continue to live at home. Ms. Brown had seen Brenda a few times in the community with her dad, and she seemed happy. Brenda engaged in recreational activities, was active in church practices, and seemed content to live at home.

This situation became a lesson for Ms. Brown, who realized that the potential of students is not always the potential that they see or that their parents have for their child. While this seemingly stunting of the development of independence can occur, educators just want students to live happy lives . . . to whatever medium that might be.

CRITICAL REFLECTIVE QUESTIONS

1. Brenda's story offers options for educators to consider regarding various types of parenting styles. What were the major ethical dilemmas regarding the expectations for Brenda from the school staff and her parents?
2. What strategies can be used for a student who refuses to complete any tasks in the classroom?

ACADEMIC LITERATURE CONNECTIONS

Billingsley, G. (2016). Combating work refusal using research-based practices. *Intervention in School and Clinic, 52*(1), 12–16.

Fingerman, K., Cheng, Y., Wesselmann, E., Zarit, S., Furstenberg, F., & Birditt, K. (2012). Helicopter parents and landing pad kids: Intense parental support of grown children. *Journal of Marriage and Family, 74*(4), 880–896.

IX

Equity Issue: Bullying

27

BULLYING VERSUS PEER INFLUENCE

When to Get Involved in the Life
of a Vulnerable Student

Amanda Zbacnik

It is often said that educators cannot make two students become friends. The challenge lies in helping students with disabilities understand the qualities that true friends possess. This vignette follows Cade from tenth through twelfth grade through peer influence situations, including a party situation that could have been life or death.

VIGNETTE #27: CADE

Ms. Brown taught Cade in tenth through twelfth grades. Cade was very intelligent in the areas of math and reading, but he struggled emotionally and behaviorally to connect positively with his peers. He was the type of student whom all the others in the special education room looked up to and wanted to be like because Cade had the coolest clothes, the newest version of the iPhone, and the good looks that allowed him to have a long-term girlfriend. Cade was also very successful with work experience, where he worked at Super One Foods stocking shelves and providing customer assistance.

The one frightening incident that is related to Cade has to do with peer influence and not being able to judge who your true friends are. When coming back to school on a Monday morning, Ms. Brown saw Cade's mother waiting for her by the classroom door. Ms. Brown could see from the tears brimming around her eyes that she had something really important to share.

She told Ms. Brown that, in an attempt for Cade to try to make new friends, he was invited to a party over the weekend where his "friends" kept offering him cup after cup of alcohol. Cade's mother's Saturday evening consisted of hearing someone knocking on her front door and opening the door to see Cade lying on his back, still as can be, on the front lawn.

Cade's "friends" had dropped him off on the lawn, knocked on the door, and simply driven away. Cade had to be brought to the emergency room and have his stomach pumped due to the large amount of alcohol that he had consumed. Cade wanted friends and to be considered cool and hang out with his general education peers so much that he didn't realize his "friends" were actually making fun of him.

His mother was shaken to the core. This could have been a life or death situation. To this day, Ms. Brown is so thankful that that night did not turn out worse than it already was and that Cade continues to live in this work-a-day world and is happy.

For the past three years, Ms. Brown has received Christmas cards from Cade's mother, offering thanks and telling her about what Cade's doing. All of his real-world involvement includes working for a cabinet company, living in an apartment with his girlfriend, and buying his first "new to him" GM car. In all aspects of life, Cade is really making it.

CRITICAL REFLECTIVE QUESTIONS

1. Having a sense of belonging is a human need. Couple this desire with vulnerability challenges stemming from a disability, and scary situations can occur. What can teachers do to educate their students about drugs, alcohol, and understanding what it means to have a true friend?

2. Cade, when asked by school administration to provide names of the "friends" who dropped him off on his front lawn, refused to share. If overhearing students talking or joking about this situation, how would you respond?

3. What does success after high school look like?

ACADEMIC LITERATURE CONNECTIONS

McLeod, D., Jones, R., & Cramer, E. (2015). An evaluation of a school-based, peer facilitated, healthy relationship program for at-risk adolescents. *Children & Schools, 37*(2), 108–116.

Vessey, J., & O'Neill, K. (2011). Helping students with disabilities better address teasing and bullying situations: A MASNRN study. *Journal of School Nursing, 27*(2), 139–148.

28

TEACHING STUDENTS WITH SPECIAL NEEDS ABOUT SEX

Who Should Do This?

Amanda Zbacnik

This vignette highlights a situation where Adam, a particularly vulnerable eleventh-grade student with an intellectual disability, is prompted by a neuro-typical peer (bully) to ask a female student to engage in sexual activity with him. What follows is a scanning of the school cameras to view the interaction between Adam and the girl and a meeting in the principal's office.

VIGNETTE #28: ADAM

Adam was one of four foster children who had disabilities and lived under the same roof. Adam was an easy-to-like type of student, always willing to help and was such a hard worker. When Adam came to high school, he was reading at a kindergarten and sometimes preprimer level. It became abundantly obvious that Adam would need a lot of training and functional work skills throughout his school day.

Due to having an intellectual disability, Adam was vulnerable around his peers. He wanted to fit in so badly that he would often be found showing others pictures of women he had cut out of magazines in their underwear or bikinis. He was also the high school student who was constantly offering up high fives and hugs. There was a definite learning curve that Ms. Brown helped Adam see when helping him understand who his true friends were and those who might be trying to pick on his vulnerabilities.

In addition to having an intellectual disability, Adam struggled to speak in a manner that was coherent. This was a real challenge to those trying to understand what he wanted. But Ms. Brown, through the sheer amount of time spent with him, understood Adam. This was a reflection of the notion that people who spend the most time with those with communication challenges have a much easier time picking up or reading into what the student is asking.

The most challenging and difficult aspect of Adam not being able to clearly communicate was brought to the forefront when his "friends" set him up in a situation that could be viewed as sexual harassment. One of the boys in Adam's grade told Adam, after slipping a condom into Adam's hand, to approach a girl and say, "Hey, let's have sex." Obviously, the girl approached in the situation did not think this was funny whatsoever and reported this to the principal.

In the events that followed, Ms. Brown had to sit down and have a conversation with Adam on why this action was not appropriate. Adam was very upset about the situation and could not understand how what he had said was wrong. He couldn't perceive how his "buddy" could tell him to do something hurtful to someone else. Adam also refused to provide us with the name of his "buddy." Loyalty was one of his assets.

Ms. Brown spent about an hour with the principal looking at the school video camera. We followed Adam through each of his steps in the hallway during the morning classes (during which the girl had reported the interaction). We were able to pinpoint a screen that showed his "buddy" handing him the pink condom that Adam later gave to the female student.

After the lengthy viewing of camera footage, the "buddy" was called into the principal's office, and justice was served.

CRITICAL REFLECTIVE QUESTIONS

1. The rules of physical contact can be challenging for students with special needs to understand and even more difficult to comprehend for those with a history of abuse. What strategies dealing with

teaching physical and social boundaries could be implemented to help Adam?

2. Educators who spend a lot of the school day with students having communication difficulties are often able to understand the message the student is trying to send. What concern, for individuals with limited speech, does this present for life after high school?

3. The condom situation is an example of bullying. What sorts of consequences are appropriate for the bully? How can educators work together to protect their most vulnerable students?

ACADEMIC LITERATURE CONNECTIONS

Hernan, C., Morrison, J., Collins, T., & Kroeger, S. (2018). Decreasing inappropriate mobile device use in middle and high school classrooms. *Intervention in School and Clinic, 54*(1), 47–51.

Shah, N. (2011). Bullying and students with disabilities, "Walk a mile in their shoes: Bullying and children with special needs." *Education Week, 30*(22), 5.

CONCLUDING REMARKS
Ethical Educators for All Students

It is our hope that this book is impactful in that it prepares teachers or any other individual(s) working with students in controversial situations to successfully navigate through challenging situations in the school environment. Being that a career in education is indeed a "practice," vignette-driven reflections can be a means of being proactive in understanding options in responding to ethical dilemmas before these events occur in classrooms.

While no author can prepare educators to comprehensively address all challenges that may occur in the classroom, this book shares twenty-eight dilemmas that were instrumental in the ideological formation of the authors, who were once educators in the field.

The sheer number of issues in the classroom may, at times, seem insurmountable. For example, within the vignettes discussed in this book, equity issues arose of parental involvement, accusations about a teacher's ability, hygiene considerations, and conflicting religious views when teaching sex education, to name a few. However, one cannot contest that being in the classroom and working through ethical challenges in the moment provides the optimal learning experience.

Thus, the questions are: Are there other methods that can come close to gaining this knowledge, without being at the expense of vulnerable children's schooling experiences in real classrooms? Another means of bridging theory to practice? The answer lies in mentally preparing for possible situations by reading, critically discussing, and collaboratively researching positive ways to address and manage different situations. Case study analysis, next to the actual practice, has been proven to provide a palatable option.

As time elapses, the need to adjust and readjust to new movements in education arises. During these times of transformation, skill sets, materials, assessments, theories, shifts of power, and literature are integral to remaining grounded in real-world classroom connections. This transformation begins with the education of those expected to implement the changes.

K–12 schools need transformational leaders, and it is exciting to know that leaders are not born; they are made (based on the fact that behaviors can be learned). Each school faculty member brings to the environment a variety of personalities, cognitive abilities, skills, motives, and expertise. Any one of these leadership qualities can be instrumental to solving complex ethical dilemmas or leading organizational change.

Being that these vignettes present very specific situations, it is important to consider that one of the most powerful leadership techniques is to simply diversify one's perspective and learn to consider multiple perspectives, based on all those who are affected by the given case.

Other ways that transformational leaders can inspire future educators is to share their stories, not only stories of success, but stories of failure too. Most often, learning occurs during times of trial and error, and as such there needs to be space and patience for educators as they develop their knowledge in addressing ethical dilemmas. In education, this can include slight tugging on the emotional "heart strings" of educators, as educators are seen to be idealized as empathetic role models for young students.

Transformational leaders teach others to approach situations via logical and rational approaches. This may involve analyzing a school's mission, root causes of the problem, acknowledging stereotypes, and determining what the student needs to succeed. Lastly, we hope that, by working through this book with a discussion-based collaborative and constructive approach, we can invite various perspectives and reframe future teachers' mindsets.

For the career of an educator, this book is significant in its versatility and alignment to instructional theory. It provides explicit guidance on how to better help people learn and develop their skills related to their students' cognitive, emotional, social, physical, and spiritual abilities (Reigeluth, 1999). The vignettes do this by going beyond simply memorizing information and inviting readers to understand the relationships in the scenarios and apply their own theoretical or lived skills to finding a solution.

In terms of relationships, readers are allowed to analyze interactions between the student and individuals involved in their lives. Additional analysis of relationships to nonhuman items also surface in terms of student access (or lack thereof) to tools, information, support systems, and manipulatives in their environments.

In terms of instructional design, this book provides learners with the opportunity to engage actively and reflectively in thoughtful practice. This can be achieved through a variety of means, as a self-assessment, to read as a motivation to derive a solution to a real-world situation (perhaps that an educator is currently experiencing), or for communities of practice to engage in the vignette questions through open and candid discussion.

This book can be used by aspiring and practicing teachers as a resource in teacher preparation courses, a resource for newly hired teachers to work through with their assigned mentor, and/or to provide professional development opportunity for all teachers. We believe that support for new teachers comes in multiple forms, such as research-based articles, case studies, critical and reflective questions, and the five-step analysis framework process specifically chosen to guide readers in responding to and analyzing the vignettes.

Confidence and openness to learning is an important component of classroom management. Along with confidence, having flexibility in one's cognition, to consider a dilemma from the perspective of multiple stakeholders in the life of a child, is also essential. Additionally, some of the variables that can make situations all the more challenging in the life of a student include neuro-diversity, developmental capabilities being below or more advanced than that of a child's same-aged peers, a variety of parenting styles, and available monetary or personnel-driven resources available in multiple school environments.

There are limitless equity issues that a teacher may need to have the courage to confront during their career in education. Our hope is that having the ability to think about a situation from a comprehensive view begins with an individual educator practicing this and that, and once observed by others, this critical thinking and decision-making model is adopted by as many educators as possible. It is truly the authors' intention that critical reflection in the education field can have the greatest impact on the greatest number of students possible.

And ultimately, all decisions effective educators make should be driven by the desire to assist their students in developing into contributing members of society. In our final remarks, we want the readers of this book to know that you will run into your past students from time to time.

Whether it's the man with autism working at the Holiday gas station with his mother, a young adult with Down syndrome riding through the Labor Day parade in support of his mother's election campaign, the once "nonverbal" female student exploring the aquarium with her boyfriend, or the man with vulnerability issues now holding down a job and living independently, all of these individuals were once assisted through challenging situations by educational staff just like you, and for this you are cherished in our minds.

We want to thank you as the future unsung heroes that work with students on a daily basis in ethically complex situations. You will help students realize their potential and provide the scaffolding needed to help them build independent living skills. We hope that, after reading this book, you will connect what you knew and what you now know with what you do.

Never underestimate the powerful impact that you have on diverse students of all races, genders, sexual orientation, and abilities. While at times it may seem like students' progress comes with minimal success, it is this progression of overcoming barrier after barrier that shapes them into the empathetic adults of our future.

REFERENCE

Reigeluth, C. M. (ed.). (1999). *Instructional-design theories and models: A new paradigm of instructional theory*. Mahwah, NJ: Lawrence Erlbaum.

ABOUT THE AUTHORS

Dr. Manu Sharma, PhD, is an assistant professor at Thompson Rivers University in the Faculty of Education and Social Work, where she currently teaches required foundational courses in the Masters of Education Program. Recently, Manu taught at the University of Wisconsin-River Falls where she taught courses that were to meet the expectations of American cultural diversity, which focus on equity and diversity issues in education. Dr. Sharma has also taught a variety of undergraduate and graduate courses and supported field placements at Brock University, University of Toronto, and University of Windsor.

In addition, she has also worked for the Toronto District School Board and in international settings, such as Japan, Antigua, Barbuda, Germany, and Tanzania as a public educator. Her research interests and publications in the field of teacher education are based on equity initiatives, teacher development, social justice pedagogy, deficit thinking, and international teaching experiences. Dr. Sharma has recently published in the *Alberta Journal of Educational Research, Journal on Excellence in College Teaching, Education and Urban Society*, and *Teacher Learning and Professional Development*.

Dr. Amanda Zbacnik, EdD, is currently an assistant professor at University of Wisconsin-Superior with extensive experience teaching special education in the public school setting. Dr. Zbacnik has worked with individuals identified as having special needs in multiple disability categories: intellectual disabilities, other health impairments, emotional/behavioral disorders, specific learning disabilities, autism, and multiple disabilities. Within these categories, she has worked with a variety of disorders: schizophrenia, Down syndrome, hearing impairment, Tay Sachs disease, fetal alcohol spectrum disorder, and more.

In addition, she has worked with students with special needs in all grades from K–12, with a primary focus at the high school level. Working at the high school level allowed Dr. Zbacnik to place an emphasis on transitions for students with special needs that required collaboration from multiple stakeholders (social workers, rights advocates, physical therapists, paraprofessionals, speech-language pathologists, parents, transition service programs, work experience coordinators, group home coordinators, etc.).

Most recently, in the summer of 2018, Dr. Zbacnik spent her time volunteering as a conditioner and side walker at North Country Ride (Find Your Stride). This organization is an equine therapy program that focuses on building individuals with disabilities' (particularly in the categories of autism and orthopedic impairment) self-confidence and core muscular strength through the riding experience. Helping a student with special needs to be successful is truly a team effort!

Dr. Zbacnik also has experience with co-teaching (the purest form of collaboration). Amanda has co-taught with speech-language pathologists for a number of years and, as a practicing special educator, built a partnership with a special education professor, bridging ideas of theory and practice. Dr. Zbacnik devoted her dissertation work to this topic. Her dissertation is titled *Co-Teaching in Higher Education: Effects on Pre-Service Educators' Academic Growth and Attitudes towards Inclusion in Special Education.*

Printed in the USA
CPSIA information can be obtained
at www.ICGtesting.com
LVHW041132150923
758081LV00005B/109